my revisi●n notes

Edexcel B GCSE
GEOGRAPHY

UNIT 2: PEOPLE AND THE PLANET

Nigel Yates

HODDER
EDUCATION
AN HACHETTE UK COMPANY

This material has been endorsed by Edexcel and offers high quality support for the delivery of Edexcel qualifications. Edexcel endorsement does not mean that this material is essential to achieve any Edexcel qualification, nor does it mean that this is the only suitable material available to support any Edexcel qualification. No endorsed material will be used verbatim in setting any Edexcel examination and any resource lists produced by Edexcel shall include this and other appropriate texts. While this material has been through an Edexcel quality assurance process, all responsibility for the content remains with the publisher. Copies of official specifications for all Edexcel qualifications may be found on the Edexcel website www.edexcel.com.

The Publishers would like to thank the following for permission to reproduce copyright material:

Photo credits: p23 *all* © Robert Gray; **p24** *t* © Reidos/Fotolia, *b* © Alex Yeung/Fotolia; **p28** © Staff/Reuters/Corbis; **p35** © JP Laffont/Sygma/Corbis; **p38** © So-Shan Au; **p46** © Jim/Fotolia; **p58** © James Boardman/Alamy.

Acknowledgements: p38 BBC news (news.bbc.co.uk); **p57** Global Footprint Network (footprintnetwork.org); **p58** Honister Mine (www.honister.com); **p22** *International Living* magazine, 2010; **p59** Lake District National Park Authority; **p58** Low Sizergh Farm (www.lowsizerghbarn. co.uk); **p23** Red Shoes blog (redshoesllc.typepad.com); **p41** Stockholm Environment Institute (www.resource-accounting.org.uk); **p77** Techworld (www.techworld.com); **p19** United Nations Human Development Index; **p20** United Nations Population Division; United Nations, *Our Common Future*, 1987.

Every effort has been made to trace all copyright holders, but if any have been inadvertently overlooked the Publishers will be pleased to make the necessary arrangements at the first opportunity.

Although every effort has been made to ensure that website addresses are correct at time of going to press, Hodder Education cannot be held responsible for the content of any website mentioned in this book. It is sometimes possible to find a relocated web page by typing in the address of the home page for a website in the URL window of your browser.

Hachette UK's policy is to use papers that are natural, renewable and recyclable products and made from wood grown in sustainable forests. The logging and manufacturing processes are expected to conform to the environmental regulations of the country of origin.

Orders: please contact Bookpoint Ltd, 130 Milton Park, Abingdon, Oxon OX14 4SB. Telephone: (44) 01235 827827. Fax: (44) 01235 400401. Lines are open 9.00–5.00, Monday to Saturday, with a 24-hour message answering service. Visit our website at www.hoddereducation.co.uk

© Nigel Yates 2012

First published in 2012 by

Hodder & Stoughton Limited,

An Hachette UK Company

338 Euston Road

London NW1 3BH

Impression number	5 4 3 2
Year	2016 2015 2014 2013 2012

Cover photo © Anatoly Maslennikov

Illustrations by Gray Publishing

Typeset in 11/13pt Stempel Schneidler Std and produced by Gray Publishing, Tunbridge Wells

Printed in India

A catalogue record for this title is available from the British Library

ISBN: 978 1444 164 497

Contents and revision planner

Unit 2 People and the Planet

Revised **Section A:** People and the Planet (compulsory topics)   4

☐ Chapter 1 Population Dynamics   4

☐ Chapter 2 Consuming Resources   13

☐ Chapter 3 Living Spaces   22

☐ Chapter 4 Making a Living   31

Revised **Section B:** Small-scale People and the Planet (optional topics – study one)   41

☐ Chapter 5 Changing Cities   41

☐ Chapter 6 Changing Countryside   51

Revised **Section C:** Large-scale People and the Planet (optional topics – study one)   61

☐ Chapter 7 Development Dilemmas   61

☐ Chapter 8 World of Work   70

Section A People and the Planet
Chapter 1 Population Dynamics
How and why is population changing in different parts of the world?

The past, present and future of global population — Revised

- The world's population was under a billion in 1750 and had only climbed to two billion by 1930. By 2011, it had grown to nearly seven billion. But look at the population increase for each 10-year period.
- The global growth rate peaked in the 1980s with over 80 million added each year in that decade. Since then the numbers 'added' each year have fallen.
- It is predicted that by the 2040s the average increase in global population will be down to 30 million a year. That is still the same as the population of the UK every two years.

Figure 1 Global population change

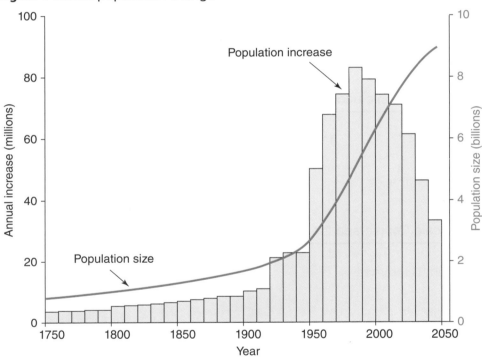

Knowing the basics

Remember that predictions about future changes are just educated guesses based on current trends. They have sometimes been very wrong in the past.

Stretch and challenge

Don't forget that the population is still growing even though the rate of growth of population might slow down.

Check your understanding — Tested

1 Which was the peak decade for global population increase?

2 Is global population growth ...
   a getting faster?
   b getting slower?

Why does population change?

The global population changes because of changes in birth rates and death (mortality) rates.

- **Birth rate** is the number of children born per 1000 of the population in a year.
- **Death rate** is the number of people who die per 1000 of the population in a year.
- The **natural increase** of a population is the difference between the birth and death rates. So if the birth rate is 40 per 1000 and the death rate 20 per 1000, the population is increasing at 20 per 1000 or two per cent every year.

examiner tip

The study of population is known as **demography**. So if a question asks for 'demographic' changes, these are changes in population.

Knowing the basics

For a country, the change in population should also include the **migration** rate – the number of people arriving and leaving a country during a year.

Here are some other useful ways of measuring population:

- **Life expectancy**: the average age at which people die in a population.
- **Infant mortality**: the number of children under the age of one year who die per 1000 births in a year.
- **Fertility rate**: the number of children that women have in their lifetime. If women have two children or more they 'replace' the parents. Fewer than two children means that the population will eventually fall.

Figure 2 Fertility rates around the world

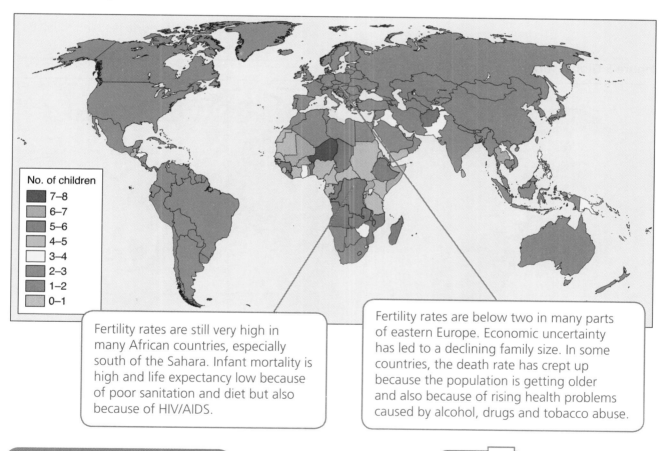

No. of children
- 7–8
- 6–7
- 5–6
- 4–5
- 3–4
- 2–3
- 1–2
- 0–1

Fertility rates are still very high in many African countries, especially south of the Sahara. Infant mortality is high and life expectancy low because of poor sanitation and diet but also because of HIV/AIDS.

Fertility rates are below two in many parts of eastern Europe. Economic uncertainty has led to a declining family size. In some countries, the death rate has crept up because the population is getting older and also because of rising health problems caused by alcohol, drugs and tobacco abuse.

Check your understanding

1 Define the term 'natural increase'.
2 Suggest ONE possible reason why natural increase might rise in a country.

Comparing countries

Revised

Many differences in population changes can be seen around the world. In some countries the population is growing rapidly; others suffer from population loss. This is because of:

- differences in birth rates
- differences in death rates
- differences in the numbers of people migrating in and out of the country.

There are many reasons for these differences, but they can be divided into the following categories:

- Economic: birth rate varies because of differences in the costs and benefits of having children. Developed societies have more resources to ensure a healthier population; better diet, better sanitation and better health care all combine to reduce death rates.

- Social: the status of women and their education are among the most important factors affecting birth rates. The impact of drugs, alcohol and crime has led to rising death rates in some eastern European countries, while religious beliefs and cultural attitudes have been factors in the spread of HIV/AIDS.

- Political: governments can make a big difference to birth rates and death rates. This is not just by their direct actions (such as China's well-known 'one-child policy') but also indirectly by the way in which they spend money on hospitals, health care, education and many other areas. They also play a key role in controlling the number of people who are allowed into a country.

Knowing the basics

The main reason for variations in birth rates is the varying costs of having children.

Stretch and challenge

Don't forget that countries with **ageing populations** may have an increasing death rate just because people are getting older.

Richer, **developed countries** tend to have lower population growth.

Figure 3 Global variations in population growth

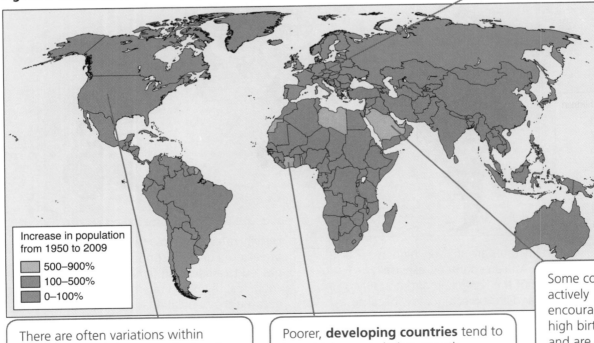

Increase in population from 1950 to 2009

- 500–900%
- 100–500%
- 0–100%

There are often variations within countries mainly because of migration.

Poorer, **developing countries** tend to have higher population growth.

Some countries actively encourage a high birth rate and are also rich enough to reduce death rates. These are the fastest growing societies.

Check your understanding

Tested

1 Which continent has the highest population growth?

2 Suggest TWO reasons why developed countries have lower death rates.

Population structures

Some countries are ageing rapidly. In most cases this is because of falling birth rates. Japan is a well-known case study, as shown in Figure 4.

Ageing populations can be difficult for countries because of:

- rising costs of health care
- rising costs of pensions
- falling numbers of 'workers' to pay taxes to fund pensions or health care.

Knowing the basics

An ageing population is one where the average age is rising.

Figure 4 Birth and death rates in Japan between 1950 and 2008

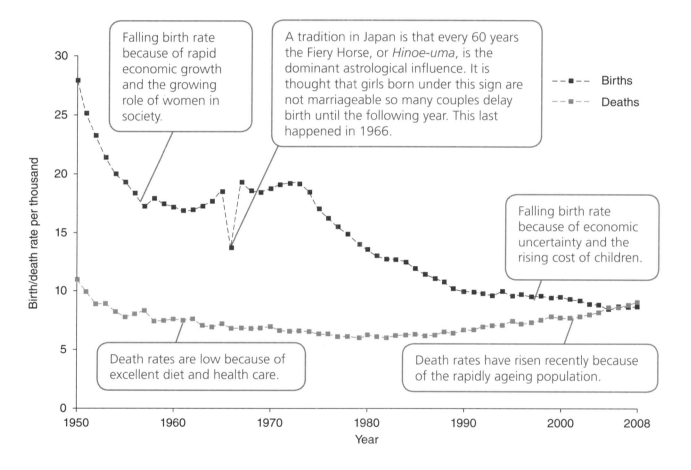

Falling birth rate because of rapid economic growth and the growing role of women in society.

A tradition in Japan is that every 60 years the Fiery Horse, or *Hinoe-uma*, is the dominant astrological influence. It is thought that girls born under this sign are not marriageable so many couples delay birth until the following year. This last happened in 1966.

Falling birth rate because of economic uncertainty and the rising cost of children.

Death rates are low because of excellent diet and health care.

Death rates have risen recently because of the rapidly ageing population.

Check your understanding

1 Identify ONE economic reason why birth rates in Japan have fallen.
2 Identify ONE reason why death rates fell until 1980.

Nigeria

Young populations can also be difficult to manage.

Nigeria has more or less the same **population structure** today that it had in 1975, with 75 per cent under the age of 30. Despite its wealth from oil, most of the population is very poor. The costs of feeding this population and funding its education are high.

The total fertility rate remains extremely high. Only eight per cent of married women of reproductive age use a modern method of contraception, partially because they want large families. Several things explain this desired fertility, including poor child survival – one-fifth of all children born in Nigeria die before five years of age – and low educational attainment among women, 42 per cent of whom have never been to school.

Knowing the basics

In developing countries such as Nigeria women have limited opportunities – this is a cause of high birth rates.

Stretch and challenge

When women are given basic education they have more choices and fertility rate almost always falls.

Check your understanding

Tested ☐

1 Identify TWO economic impacts of an ageing population.

2 Identify TWO economic costs of a young population.

How far can population change and migration be managed sustainably?

Why do countries wish to control their populations? Revised ☐

In any country there will be a wide variety of opinions about the 'ideal' or optimum population size.

Figure 5 Relationships between population and resources

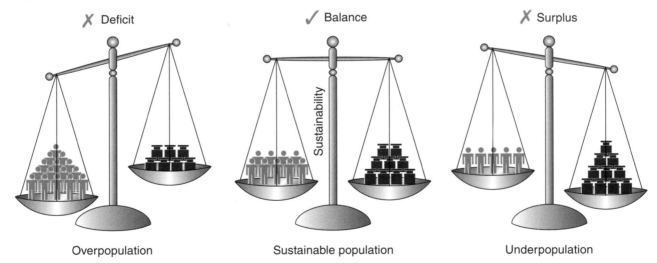

✗ Deficit   ✓ Balance   ✗ Surplus

Sustainability

Overpopulation   Sustainable population   Underpopulation

The difficulty with the concepts of **overpopulation** and **underpopulation** is that very few countries could now feed themselves or provide sufficient energy from their own resources. Almost all countries trade; for example, the UK provides finance and business services which it 'sells' and then uses that money to buy imported food and fuel. This makes the question of 'resources' much more complicated than it was in pre-industrial times.

- In the UK there are some groups that believe the country would be better off with a population of about 30 million.
- Other people believe that the UK is underpopulated.
- Governments decide on policies, although they need to be careful about popular opinion if they wish to be elected. This is especially true of migration policies, where public opinion is divided.
- Governments may also wish to control *where* people live in a country, the structure of that population, especially its age, and possibly its ethnicity.

Knowing the basics

If population grows faster than resources there will be a crisis of some sort. Famine and war are obvious possibilities.

Stretch and challenge

Ageing populations can also 'save' money for governments. They spend a lot less on children's education and maternity care.

examiner tip

- You will need to know two case studies for this section: one of a country with **anti-natal policies** that discourages large families and one with **pro-natal policies** that does the opposite.
- You may be asked to provide a few details, so learn three facts about each country.

Economic arguments	Social and political arguments
• Lack of labour to develop industries and trade This was true of the early USA. Canada and Australia are both possible candidates for this today, although this is not accepted by all Canadians or Australians	• Some governments encourage larger families because they believe that large countries are more powerful than small ones In North Korea, one of the most 'secret' countries in the world, it would appear that the government believes that the population is too small, especially when compared with South Korea
• Fears about an ageing population and the longer term economic status of a country dominated by elderly people In 2011, 23 per cent of Japan's population was over 65. Japan would need to raise its retirement age to 77 or admit one million immigrants annually between 2000 and 2050 to maintain its current ratio of workers to 'dependants'	• Other governments might believe that ethnic diversity has negative effects, so slowing down or stopping immigration and encouraging the dominant racial or religious group to have larger families

Check your understanding

Tested ☐

1 What is overpopulation?
2 What is underpopulation?

Population polices in practice

China: anti-natalist but for how long?

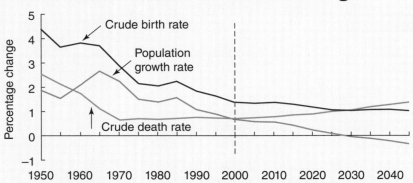

Figure 6 Trends in China's population growth rate, birth rate and death rate

Why anti-natalist?
- Population was growing very rapidly throughout the 1950s and 1960s – at that time encouraged by the government.
- New political leaders decided that a large population size was a problem.

Which policies?
- Voluntary programmes and land reform led to a sharp fall in birth rate in the 1970s.
- The famous 'one-child policy' was started in 1979. It gave benefits to women in the form of cash bonuses, better housing and maternity care. It also punished couples who did not sign up. Forced sterilisation happened in some regions of the country.

The impact?
- Birth rate continued to fall. Today China has a fertility rate of 1.7; below the replacement level of two.
- This has raised issues of China's rapidly ageing society and the impact on the single children of looking after elderly parents.
- The preference for boys (still common in many societies) led to sex-selective abortion and today there are 120 males for every 100 females.
- A 'social' impact much commented on is how spoilt the single children are – described by some as 'little emperors'.

Singapore: first anti-natalist and then pro-natalist!

- Singapore is a small, island nation. When it first became independent it pursued an anti-natal policy just as in modern China, although not quite so strictly.
- This policy was successful, and along with the impact of later marriage, rising incomes and the increased role of women in society, the fertility rate fell from 3.0 in 1970 to 1.6 in 1985.
- Today Singapore is worried that its only resource is its population so the government now tries to encourage earlier marriage and larger families.
- Couples with three or more children pay lower taxes, have better housing, easier access to nursery schools and preference in school choice later on.
- The policies have had a very limited impact in Singapore with the drive today being to get couples together in the first place. The government is so desperate it now sponsors speed-dating events.

Stretch and challenge

Many countries, such as Singapore, have few resources except their people. Population growth provides more skills if these people can be educated.

Check your understanding

1 What are anti-natalist policies?

2 What are pro-natalist policies?

Why do migration policies vary from place to place and from time to time?

Revised

Many people are hostile to immigration.

- 75 per cent of the UK's population wish to reduce immigration.
- About the same number are happy to accept migrants who have 'special skills' or can support themselves financially.

Governments, who have to decide on the policies, have to think about:

- What they think is best for the country at that time.
- What they think the public will accept.
- What international agreements they need to consider. As an example, the UK is a member of the European Union (EU) and in the same way as British citizens can retire to Spain (another member state) without permission or special paperwork from the Spanish government, so Spaniards can come to the UK.

Knowing the basics
Most countries can control migration but rarely can they prevent it altogether.

examiner tip
Make sure that you are prepared for questions that ask about why countries have different migration policies and what policies they might have. Do not get these ideas confused.

Stretch and challenge

In some years more people leave the UK than arrive there; 1992 is an example.

- Since 2000 the number of migrants to the UK has been between 500,000 and 600,000 each year – the numbers leaving have been around 400,000.
- This makes net migration about 200,000. About 40 per cent of the migrants come from EU countries. Another 40 per cent come from Commonwealth countries.
- About 40 per cent either come with a job already lined up or are accompanying these people. Another 40 per cent come to study at schools and universities. About 10 per cent come to look for work but with no job arranged in advance.

Knowing the basics
You need to know why migrants come to a country. Work is the main reason – an economic motive. Education and joining relatives are common social reasons.

Stretch and challenge
All governments know that they need some migrants to fill jobs that cannot be done as well as by the 'locals' and most know that in a globalised world there may have to be more migration in the future in order to stay competitive.

Different migration policies and their impact

Revised

Some of the commonest ways of controlling migration include:

- **Guest worker**: programmes in which migrants stay for an agreed limited time.
- **Quotas**: a limit to the numbers allowed in – these often vary from country to country.
- **Skills tests**: these are used to limit migrants arriving without the skills to add to the economy.
- **e-Borders schemes**: migrants are monitored more closely to make sure that they do not outstay the period stated on their visas.
- **Open-door policy** is a policy of not having a policy, so to speak. Just allow migrants to come and go without restriction.

Knowing the basics
Quotas and skills tests are the commonest ways of restricting numbers of migrants.

Check your understanding

Tested

1 Name TWO global locations that supply most of the migrants to the UK.
2 Identify the TWO main reasons why migrants come to the UK.
3 Define the terms: **a** Open-door policy.   **b** Skills tests.

Exam focus

1 Study Figure 1 (page 4). Describe the changes in global population shown. [2]

2 Describe the changes in the rate of global population growth in Figure 1. [3]

3 Define the term 'fertility rate'. [2]

4 Outline ONE impact of falling fertility rates. [2]

5 Study Figure 3 (page 6). Describe the pattern of population growth in South America. [2]

6 Explain TWO economic reasons why fertility rate might fall in a country. [4]

7 Describe ONE impact of an ageing population on death rates. [2]

8 For a named country, describe TWO problems of a 'young' population. [4]

9 Define the term 'underpopulation'. [2]

10 Suggest TWO economic reasons why a government might wish to control its population. [4]

11 Which of the following best describes anti-natalist policies? [1]

   A. When people decide to have fewer children.

   B. When governments encourage larger families.

   C. When governments encourage smaller families.

   D. When people decide to have more children.

12 For a named country, explain why it has pro-natalist policies. [4]

13 Outline ONE reason why countries may find it hard to limit the number of immigrants. [2]

14 Explain TWO reasons some countries might need larger numbers of immigrants. [4]

15 Which of the following best describes an 'open-door' policy? [1]

   A. A policy that lets people leave a country without any limits.

   B. A policy that encourages people to be polite to migrants.

   C. A policy that lets migrants into a country without restriction.

   D. A policy that gives all migrants jobs automatically.

16 Describe TWO ways in which a government might limit the number of immigrants. [4]

Answers online

Chapter 2 Consuming Resources

How and why does resource consumption vary in different parts of the world?

Resources can be split into three groups:

- **Natural resources**: those things found in the natural world that we are able to use.
- **Human resources**: the skills and potential of the population.
- **Material or capital resources**: goods produced in the past.

Stretch and challenge

Remember that resources have seldom run out in the past. We gave up using flint axes because we found new materials, not because we ran out of flint. Perhaps we'll still have oil in the ground when we find some other convenient form of fuel for transport.

In normal use when people refer to a country's resources they mean its 'natural' resources. The resources include the natural environment that we frequently take for granted such as water, air and soil.

Threats to natural resources are among the greatest challenges of the twenty-first century, challenges that we are currently losing.

Resources are often defined in terms of their availability:

Type of resource	Definition	Example
Non-renewable	They cannot be remade – once used they have run out forever	Oil is the best known
Sustainable and renewable	These are renewable but only if we get involved	Wood or biofuels such as soya or palm oil – renewable if we replant
Renewable	These resources sustain themselves without human intervention and, as such, are just about limitless	Solar energy or wind power are the best examples

Running out of resources often poses a challenge, but some resources are more significant than others for human survival. We are using up these basic resources at an alarming rate. A good example is soil, which is only renewable over a long period of time and is under increasing threat.

---

examiner tip

Questions on this section might often use terms like costs and benefits, so make sure that you not only understand these but also how to classify them – economic costs might be balanced by social benefits.

Using resources has costs and benefits

Exploiting resources obviously brings benefits to those who own and sell them and also to those who use them. But it also has costs, such as an impact on the environment. Sometimes these costs are long-term costs only being 'paid' in the future while the benefits might be short-term benefits, almost immediate.

Resource	Benefits	Costs
Tar-sand oil: non-renewable	• There are 300 billion barrels of oil in the tar-sands of Canada – a huge potential profit for the oil companies • The Canadian government will benefit from tax revenue from the oil companies • Dependence on unstable Middle Eastern supplies would be reduced	• Heavy oil from tar-sand produces three times the amount of greenhouse gases as conventional oil • To remove the oil from the sand, vast quantities of natural gas and water are required, polluting the groundwater • To get to the oil, the topsoil and the ancient forests have to be stripped off completely
Biofuels: renewable and sustainable *These include ethanol produced from corn and biodiesel produced from palm oil and soya*	• Although carbon dioxide is produced when they are burned as fuel, they capture it while they grow • Countries can became more self-sufficient given the variety of crops available, so making them more secure • Biofuels can be used without much modification to vehicle engines	• The intensive farming methods used actually release a lot of carbon dioxide • To produce enough fuel for all the vehicles in the UK, the whole of the UK's agricultural land would have to be used • Growing just one crop reduces habitat variety – biofuel crops are leading to loss of rainforest
Solar power: sustainable/ unlimited	• Solar power is unlimited, widely available and 'free' • It has very low costs for the environment with very low carbon dioxide emissions • New, thinner solar panels and other technical changes promise much cheaper production in the future	• It cannot produce power at night time or in cloudy weather so you need a back-up system too • Solar panels are expensive and unless subsidised they do not pay for themselves • To produce significant amounts of power, huge areas would need to be covered with panels

Knowing the basics

Most of the costs and benefits are economic but some are environmental – try to use these terms.

examiner tip

You need to know why the **consumption** and production of one resource varies across the world. It doesn't need to be oil.

Stretch and challenge

Remember that costs and benefits fall unevenly. The individuals and companies who benefit from the profits of tar-sand 'mining' do not generally live in the region which is having its environment polluted and ultimately destroyed.

Resources are unevenly distributed and unevenly consumed

Production

It is easier to explain uneven production than consumption. Three factors explain most of the variation in production:

Reason	Example
Geography and geology	• Saudi Arabia is the world's largest producer of crude oil because the country sits on the largest reserves • If you haven't got it, you cannot produce it. This explains most of the variations in supply
Technology and exploration	• Some resources require quite expensive technology both to find and produce • Siberian gas supplies are a good example, as are deepwater oil supplies, where a mistake leading to drilling a 'dry hole' can be extremely costly – up to $200 million according to BP, an oil company
Political decisions	• Some methods of extracting fossil fuels and other materials are very damaging • Tar-oil is one example, but other examples include 'mountain-top' coal mining and 'fracking' to exploit natural gas • Attitudes and laws regarding these environmentally damaging methods vary

Consumption

About 20 per cent of the world's population – mostly living in developed countries – consume 86 per cent of the world's resources. For some resources this is even more uneven.

Knowing the basics

Wealthy, developed countries consume much more oil because they have more cars, more consumer goods and more expensive lifestyles.

Figure 1 Oil consumption around the world

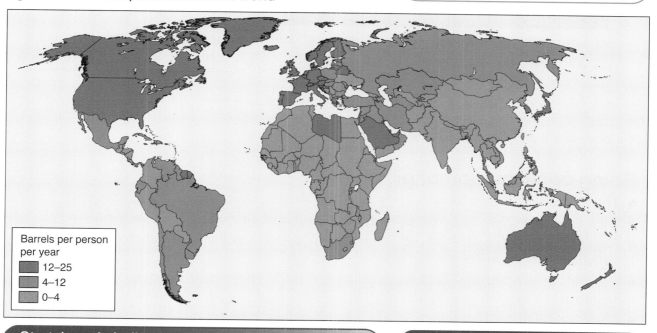

Barrels per person per year
- 12–25
- 4–12
- 0–4

Stretch and challenge

Large countries with large populations consume a lot of oil although individual consumption will be quite low. Rapidly growing economies consume increasing amounts.

Stretch and challenge

Poorer, developing countries have very low levels of car ownership. 70 per cent of oil is used for transport – cars, ships and planes. Africa's total consumption is three million barrels a day, although there are three times as many people as in the USA.

Stretch and challenge

Some countries consume a great deal of oil because they produce it very cheaply – people may not all be wealthy but petrol is cheap. Saudis can buy 15 litres for the same price as 1 litre in the UK.

The future pressures on supply and consumption

'Peak oil' is high on the list of the many threats that currently challenge us. A lot of people think that we are coming to the end of the era of cheap oil, when oil is produced for as little as $1 for a barrel (a barrel is about 160 litres or 35 gallons) in contrast to the production costs of Canadian tar-sands which are around $40 a barrel (without including the costs of any environmental damage).

The problem is shown graphically in Figure 2.

Figure 2 Oil production since 1965 and forecast to 2015

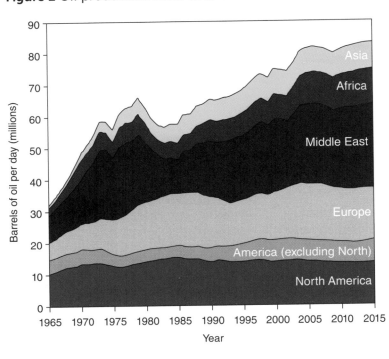

Knowing the basics

Global oil production is beginning to slow down. Most parts of the world have seen very limited increases in production in recent years with a fall in several regions.

Stretch and challenge

Some regions may increase production because of the exploitation of more expensive oil such as tar-sands in Canada.

Stretch and challenge

The only global region expected to increase production significantly is the Middle East but this is a very unstable region politically.

Despite problems of supply now and in the future, consumption is rising quickly. The issue here is the demand for oil from the emerging economies of China and India as well as Brazil, Russia and others.

Rising consumption of oil

- The Chinese and Indians hope to enjoy the same lifestyles as Europeans and Americans.
- Oil is used to produce many goods as well as providing the power to transport them.
- Rising demand for cars and other consumer goods will obviously add to carbon dioxide emissions in both production and use.
- Currently 25 per cent of global oil is consumed by the USA – it has five per cent of the world's population.
- There is no evidence that Americans are prepared to reduce their use of oil.
- There is increasing political pressures as countries try to negotiate deals with oil-producing countries. China had built alliances with many African oil producers. Resource wars are a distinct possibility with consumption rising and production flat-lining.

Knowing the basics

By 2050 the Chinese will have incomes of about 40 per cent of American incomes. The Indians will be 20 per cent as well off. This will massively increase demand.

Stretch and challenge

If China's and India's car ownership matches their increased wealth in 2050, there will be another 700 million more cars on the roads of these countries. That is double the current number.

How sustainable is the current pattern of resource supply and consumption?

Theories about population and resources

Revised ☐

Malthus (1766–1834)

- It seems obvious that as the population grows the fewer resources we will have. Thomas Malthus concluded this over 200 years ago.
- He suggested that population would grow by doubling: 2, 4, 8, 16, 32 and so on, but food production would only increase singly: 2, 3, 4, 5, 6 and so on.
- Obviously enough a gap would appear between the two and food shortages would lead to a series of social and economic crises with an eventual collapse of the population.
- Malthus was proved wrong by the astonishing advances in food production in the nineteenth century, a trend that continued into the twentieth century with the 'green revolution' and into the twenty-first century with the development of genetically modified (GM) crops.

Figure 3 A graph showing **Malthus' basic theory**

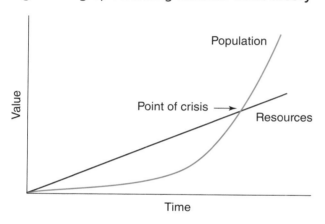

Knowing the basics

When population is larger than the resources available there will be conflict, disease and famine.

Stretch and challenge

Modern Malthusians are less troubled by population growth but more worried about the uneven pattern of consumption with rich countries consuming so much.

Stretch and challenge

Malthus was a member of the rich aristocracy who owned most of the land. He wrote his book to persuade people not to give welfare support to poor people – known as the poor law.

Boserup (1910–1999)

- Ester Boserup took a very different view to Malthus.
- The rapid growth of the human population in the past two centuries does pose a challenge for Malthusians. Boserup suggested that we never run out of resources because as we get to the point when resources are getting short we are pressured to invent ways of avoiding a crisis.
- For Boserup, a growing population *causes* changes in technology that allow the population to grow again. This makes population growth absolutely central to the development of the human species.

Figure 4 A graph showing **Boserup's theory**

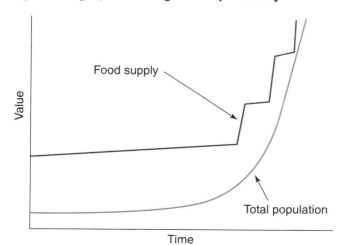

Knowing the basics

'Necessity is the mother of invention.' Population growth leads to changes in technology allowing the population to grow again.

Stretch and challenge

Boserup believed that population grows because we make changes in technology. In her view, the 'green revolution' and the development of GM crops are *results* of population growth.

Is population growth a threat?

The twenty-first century view

The greatest problem for the Malthusians is that the last two centuries have seen global population grow from about one billion when Thomas Malthus developed his theory to something approaching seven billion today, with incomes rising too.

Of course, there is a great deal of poverty – actually very many more than one billion people are living in poverty, but as a percentage poverty has declined.

The problems for people who follow Boserup's view are as follows:

● Just because technical changes have happened in the past there is no reason to assume that they will continue to do so in the future.

● Every major ecosystem on the planet is in decline – from coral reefs to mangroves to taiga to tundra – we are in serious trouble.

● Basic resources are in difficulty. We might replace oil with the hydrogen economy; other power sources may be produced but air, soil and water are under pressure.

There is a real problem here about a conflict between different goals to achieve sustainability (see Figure 5).

Knowing the basics

Malthus was proved wrong by the growth in food output and wealth in the nineteenth and twentieth centuries.

Stretch and challenge

In reality Malthus was only concerned about the growth of the 'poor' population. He was worried about a revolution.

Knowing the basics

● **Economic development** is about meeting the material needs of present and future generations.
● **Social progress** is about allowing people to fulfil their hopes and wishes.
● **Environmental responsibility** is about preserving ecosystems.

Figure 5 One view of sustainability

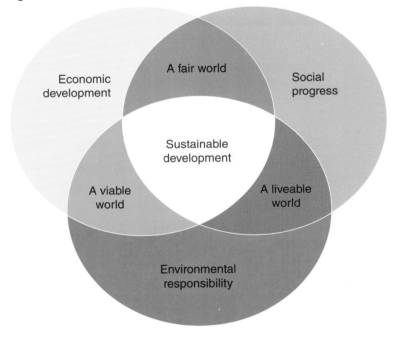

Stretch and challenge

Economic development is bound to use resources and produce waste – raising the present generation of poor people to reasonable living standards will be hard to achieve without damaging the environment.

Economic growth in the past 30 years has widened the gap between rich and poor both within and between countries – this has not helped social unity or international relations.

Looking after the environment is very hard to achieve while increasing output. If people in China and India wish to own cars and achieve this goal, carbon dioxide emissions are certain to rise!

A useful way of measuring resource consumption is the **eco-footprint**. This measures the amount of land needed to support a particular lifestyle. This includes what we consume, our travel and our production of waste.

Figure 6 The eco-footprint of selected continents and countries

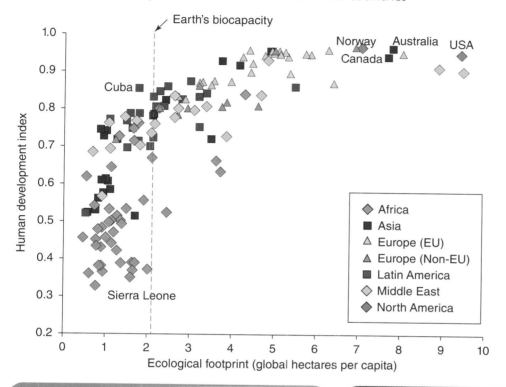

examiner tip

The eco-footprint is a very useful idea when answering questions but you will not be asked to define the term.

Knowing the basics

Rich, developed countries are responsible for the majority of the global footprint. Poor, developing countries hardly use any resources. The overall message: it's up to the rich, developed world to reduce consumption.

Stretch and challenge

Reducing eco-footprints will not be easy. Few people want to contemplate consuming less. An economic recession which reduces consumption is considered a sign of 'failure' for a government.

There are two ways of reducing our footprints:

- Reducing our consumption both as individuals and as countries.
- Making products more efficiently by using more sustainable materials and with less waste.

Changing our lifestyles (individual)

- Take public transport and give up using your own car.
- Eat only raw food.
- Use low-energy light bulbs.
- Turn down the thermostat on heating.
- Reduce water use to a minimum.

Changing production methods

Interface Carpets is a company trying to reduce its impact on the environment. The company will:

- obtain all of its energy from renewable sources by 2020
- install renewable energy systems
- measure, reduce and compensate for carbon emissions
- sell 'carbon neutral' products
- motivate workers with waste reduction programmes.

The prospects for a switch to alternative and renewable resources

Revised ☐

The full definition of sustainability is taken from the United Nations report of 1987:

Sustainable development is development that meets the needs of the present without compromising [limiting] the ability of future generations to meet their own needs.

Knowing the basics

We should consume in such a way as to allow our children and grandchildren the chance to enjoy a decent lifestyle.

Stretch and challenge

Many of the present generation do not meet their most basic needs. To help them gain access to fresh water and a decent diet, quite apart from the luxuries of Western lifestyles, will require either very rapid economic growth or a major shift of wealth from rich to poor.

The most obvious problems are:

Problem	Solutions	Prospects and Challenges
Burning of fossil fuels contributing to climate change, pollution and health issues	• The hydrogen economy offers a hope • Alternative energy sources such as solar power, wind turbines • Second- and third-generation biofuels • Better technology to reduce emissions from existing sources	As economies grow so do their energy needs. China has been building new power stations, most of them coal fired, at the rate of about one a week. There are no immediate chances of this changing other than by global economic collapse. Even with these new power stations the average Chinese citizen produces only about one-third as much carbon dioxide as the average UK citizen
Food and water shortages and degradation of land	• Most of the available agricultural land is in use • Increasing food supply has involved the use of technology such as the 'green revolution' and GM crops • This has led to a huge increase in yields but also a growing use of fertilisers, pesticides and machinery • It has also led to soil erosion and desertification • Modern agriculture uses vast quantities of water resulting in serious water shortages • Recycling water is one route forward	Science and technology have helped us avoid major famines. Food crises today are largely a consequence of the inability of people to afford food and not its availability. However, many commentators are unhappy about the long-term issues of modern food production techniques. Water conservation methods are often low technology and quite simple but shifts in diet to include more meat have placed a major strain on water resources in many countries. Recycling water as practised in Singapore is expensive in energy and in some countries losses from leakage are cheaper to 'cure' by just finding new sources of supply
Waste production and its disposal	• Many industrial processes are very wasteful • The problems are often difficult to solve • One example would be the debate about nuclear power • The production of bottled water is another example	Disposing of waste is expensive and often environmentally damaging. There are interesting global links – many computers are manufactured in China and a third of computers bought in the UK return to China for recycling. Plastic waste has accumulated in the Pacific Ocean with negative long-term effects. Nuclear waste has to be stored safely for thousands of years. Technology may assist us but the current situation is getting worse

1 Define the term 'renewable resource'. [2]

2 Identify TWO renewable resources that might help replace oil. [2]

3 Which of the following is a non-renewable resource? [1]

   A. Solar energy.

   B. Biofuel.

   C. Coal.

   D. Wind power.

4 For a named resource, explain why there are costs and benefits of using it. [4]

5 State ONE reason why the production of non-renewable resources is uneven. [1]

6 Explain why developed countries use more resources than developing countries. [4]

7 Which of the following best describes 'peak oil'? [1]

   A. When oil demand rises.

   B. When oil production reaches its maximum.

   C. When oil is found in mountainous areas.

8 Outline ONE reason why the demand for oil is likely to increase. [2]

9 Study Figure 4 on page 17. State TWO possible results when population exceeds resources. [2]

10 Explain why population growth might be a good thing. [4]

11 Which of the following suggests that Ester Boserup may have been wrong? [1]

   A. Many people are better off than ever.

   B. Population growth is slowing down.

   C. Every major eco-system is in decline.

   D. Many people are poor today.

12 Outline ONE reason why economic growth might make it hard to preserve the environment. [2]

13 Study Figure 6 on page 19. Describe the relationship between the human development index and the ecological footprint of countries. [2]

14 Describe TWO ways in which individuals can reduce their ecological footprint. [4]

15 Define the term 'sustainable development'. [2]

16 Describe TWO problems created by the production of waste. [4]

Answers online

Chapter 3 Living Spaces
What are the ingredients of good living spaces?

What makes a country attractive? — Revised

International comparisons are a good starting point for determining what makes a country attractive. Polls and surveys depend a great deal on the questions asked and results are certainly not consistent. A recent survey carried out by *International Living* magazine in 2010 revealed the rank order of countries shown in Figure 1.

Figure 1 One magazine's survey showing the top places to live

Where to find *La Dolce Vita* ('the sweet life')		
1 France	10 Italy	19 Uruguay
2 Australia	11 Netherlands	20 Hungary
3 Switzerland	12 Norway	21 Portugal
4 Germany	13 Austria	22 Lithuania
5 New Zealand	14 Liechtenstein	23 Andorra
6 Luxembourg	15 Malta	24 Czech Republic
7 USA	16 Denmark	25 United Kingdom
8 Belgium	17 Spain	
9 Canada	18 Finland	

The survey judged countries by cost of living, culture and leisure, environment, safety, culture and weather.

Why is France so desirable? The publisher of the magazine commented: 'In France, life is savoured,' she said. 'I don't think anyone will argue that France is one of the most beautiful countries in the world. The French love tidy gardens, pretty sidewalk cafés, and clean streets. Cities are well tended and with little crime.'
Variety is also seen as a major factor in France's appeal; the survey noting:
'Romantic Paris offers the best of everything, but services don't fall away in Alsace's wine villages, in wild and lovely Corsica, in lavender-scented Provence. Or in the Languedoc of the troubadours, bathed in Mediterranean sunlight.'

A survey carried out by a market researcher in 2004 showed that people's definitions of what makes a place good to live are quite consistent both over time and when comparing rural and urban communities.

Figure 2 What makes a good living space?

Factor	Percentage
Low crime level	70
Health services	59
Affordable housing	58
Education	53
Public transport	52
Shopping facilities	51
Job prospects	50
Access to countryside	49
Pollution	48
Good neighbours	47

Knowing the basics
Surveys such as this one rarely record the opinions of young people. Different groups of people will have different views about what makes a **living space** attractive to live in. It depends on which stage they are in a **life cycle**.

Stretch and challenge
Older people, especially those who are retired, are unlikely to be worried about job prospects or education, at least not for themselves. They may of course be worried about their children's prospects.

examiner tip
It is important to remember that what people think places will be like – their **perception** – is often what drives their behaviour. Their perception may not be the reality. Like holiday brochures, only the best may be mapped into our hope and dreams.

The qualities of living spaces are seen through different eyes so we cannot draw up a 'list' that will apply in all situations.

Figure 3 The different factors that make living spaces more or less attractive

> Retired people are unlikely to be troubled by jobs or wage levels; young people will be very concerned. Transport links will concern the young but not wealthy commuters or retirees who drive.

> Crime rates and the quality of the heath service concern elderly people more than young people or commuters. Leisure services do matter to young people as does the quality of communication.

Economic factors
- Job availability
- Wage levels
- Transport links
- Cost of living
- House prices and availability

Social factors
- Crime rates
- Quality of health services
- Education
- Available leisure facilities
- Broadband availability
- Neighbours

How to judge living spaces

Political factors
- Stability and safety
- Opportunity to 'have a say'
- A free press
- Freedom of movement

Environmental factors
- Climate
- Water availability
- Ground conditions
- Quality of built environment
- Risk of hazards

One of most challenging living spaces in the developed world is the city of Detroit in the USA. But some people still love it.

Detroit in 'facts'

- Unemployment levels reach 50 per cent in the poorest districts.
- It has the lowest average incomes in any American city.
- It has the highest crime rate in the USA.
- It has thousands of abandoned properties with prices as low as a few hundred dollars for detached houses.
- It has higher death rates and lower life expectancy than anywhere else in the USA.
- Its population has fallen from over 2.5 million to less than one million in 40 years.
- Education levels are among the worst in the USA.
- Large areas of the city are reverting to nature.

Detroit love (from blog: http://redshoesllc. typepad.com/my_weblog/2011/04/detroit-love. html with kind permission)

I have a thing for Detroit. Maybe it's because in this day and age where everyone seems to be striving for perfection, being imperfect and full of flaws is what I find real and admirable.

- I love going around seeing the old buildings, and neighbourhoods.
- I love the music, the blues especially.
- I love the way people are thinking about the future of the city – the farms – the new ideas.
- I love the fact that it is authentic. Authenticity is far better than perfection in my book.

Town or country?

In many developed societies, especially those that passed through the industrial revolution early, such as the UK, rural life has been idealised: the 'rural idyll'. Many people think it is better than urban life, with safer and more supportive communities. In some respects they are correct.

People who live in villages live longer. There are three reasons for this: there are fewer social issues; commuter villages are often wealthy; and the countryside is healthier in general.

However, the reality is not always the same as the dream.

Not so idyllic?
- Rural populations are increasingly elderly which has an impact on services, in terms of the need for doctors, post offices, schools and transport.
- In many places over 35 per cent of the population are aged over 65.
- The loss of young people continues as they are unable to buy houses in the villages where they grew up.
- Affordable housing is in short supply and young people are priced out by older and much wealthier migrants.
- Social and leisure facilities naturally are geared to the older and more influential section of the population.

City life?
- 80 per cent of Britons live in cities.
- However, inner London and other cities are getting younger, with central city areas providing more jobs in financial and business services in recent years. These jobs generate others in supporting retail and leisure employment.

In the developing world, the most significant movement of people is the rapid shift from rural areas to urban areas, the **rush for the towns**.

Figure 4 China's urban/rural population from 1950 to 2030 (projected figures for 2010–30)

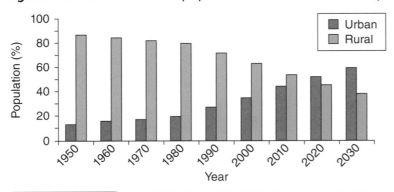

Knowing the basics

There are fewer jobs in rural China and those that remain are less well paid than those in the cities. Most jobs in manufacturing industries are in the fast-growing cities in the east, many on or close to the coast.

Stretch and challenge

There are other motives for moving to cities – education is often a key reason. There were about two million students in China in 2000, today it is close to 20 million.

examiner tip

Do not confuse changes in percentages with changes in total amounts. The population of rural China has not decreased in total numbers (absolute) but has decreased as a share of this (rising) total population.

Changing views about living spaces

The family members below all live in a village in Wiltshire:

	Opinions	Comment
Elliot – aged 10	'I love it here – it's quiet and there aren't many problems like riots – all my friends at school live close and we can go exploring together – my Nan used to live in London but I didn't like it much'	In rural areas the vast majority of 4–11 year olds will go to a village school within fairly easy reach. Most people perceive rural areas to be 'safer' for children
Mel – aged 17	'It was OK growing up here I suppose and it might get better now I can drive although I haven't got a car. It takes so long to get anywhere and my friends at school live miles away. I'm hoping to go to university next year – probably in Bath. I like it there. There are loads of things to do and places to go and it's a bit cheaper and less scary than London. And not too far from home!'	Secondary schools are larger and have wider catchments so you will have fewer school friends living locally to you. Most rural areas have poor transport services and this can lead to more social isolation for teenaged children

Knowing the basics

Remember that the choices people make about living spaces are often based on what they think places are like rather than what they are really like.

Stretch and challenge

Psychologists tell us that 'confirmation bias' means that most of us look for evidence that confirms our prejudices. If we believe Bath is less 'scary' than London we pick up on any snippets that suggest that this is true and ignore evidence that suggests the opposite.

	Opinions	Comment
Oliver – aged 22	'I graduated last year and have been working for six months in the local farm shop. Actually I've just got an internship in a city accountancy firm and will be moving back to London next week. I'm going to share a flat with three ex-uni friends in Bermondsey – I do like it here, it's home after all, but there aren't so many jobs, certainly not for new graduates and the city is pretty cool. My girlfriend works there too'	When asked where they would like to live in the future the vast majority of school leavers name their home area as their first preference. The second preference is often a nearby city or the capital city, many of which have been regenerated in recent years (re-urbanisation), offering more jobs, especially in financial services. The exception is students in remote rural regions who place these cities above their local areas
Andy – aged 47	'I was brought up in the city but changed jobs in my 20s and moved to Wiltshire – it's a great area to raise children although you act as a taxi driver for years. I do miss the 'buzz' you get from urban life from time to time but I don't miss the commuting or the stress of urban life. The local community is strong although both the pub and shop may close soon'	Counter-urbanisation and re-urbanisation are opposite movements. The return to rural areas is especially obvious when these areas are in commuting range of large urban areas. Commuting is expensive and is unusual in the 20–30 age group. Moving out of the city to the fringes and rural margin depends on high levels of car ownership
Christine – aged 70	'I moved down here two years ago to be closer to my family – my eldest son lives here. I can see the children regularly now although I miss my London friends. Before my husband died we talked a lot about moving to France but it wasn't to be. Some of my friends have moved abroad but I am not sure how happy they are; it's hard to judge, it's a big decision'	When people retire they can, within the limits of their income, choose to live wherever they wish. Cheaper property and a better climate combine with better communications and the development of air travel and the internet to make retirement overseas an appealing option. Not all find that this 'idyll' lives up to their expectations and many return home

Retirement overseas

Spain

Figure 5 Foreign residents in Spain as a percentage of the total population

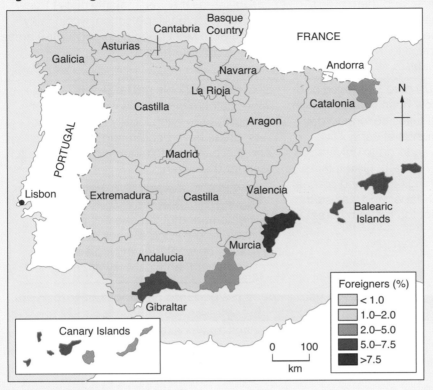

- 750,000 non-Spanish EU citizens, mostly from the UK, live on or close to the Spanish coast.
- Many of these non-Spanish EU citizens are retired – **retirement migration** is an important trend in Europe.
- Summer temperatures are 5 °C higher and winters are milder than the UK.
- House prices were traditionally as much as a third cheaper than those in the UK.
- Cheap air travel and the development of the internet have made it easier and cheaper to stay in touch with home.
- British communities have grown so there is a 'cultural' link.

However:

- Pensions have declined as the pound has fallen against the euro.
- The cost of living has risen in Spain (and France).
- Property disputes have arisen over ownership rights.
- Many retirees still feel isolated from home and with nothing to do; boredom and marital breakdown are not unusual.

How far can growing demands for good living spaces become more sustainable?

The pressure on rural areas in developed countries

There are different types of rural area and the pressures tend to be different according to how far they are from large urban areas.

Areas close to large cities are heavily affected because:

- Cities need to grow to survive so there is pressure for more houses and office space.
- City dwellers wish to move out to surrounding villages.
- Some of these do not wish for further development after they move in.
- Roads and other transport systems are likely to be under pressure.

More remote rural areas suffer because of:

- Lack of variety of jobs.
- Low wages.
- Limited educational and social opportunities for young people.

Draw up a case study table and complete it for two contrasting rural areas:

	Rural area 1	Rural area 2
Local details – fact file		
Pressures	1 2 3	1 2 3
Consequences	1 2	1 2

The causes and consequences of growing demand for urban spaces

Revised

Urban spaces are attractive because:

- they offer a wide variety of opportunities for people
- they include a wider range of jobs
- they offer better paid jobs for some
- they offer a fuller social life.

Indian cities are among the fastest growing in the developing world as the country experiences huge economic changes. India's ninth largest city, Surat, is typical. Its population, about 3.5 million in 2011, has doubled in 10 years, mostly because of migration from the countryside.

In the developed world, city growth can also be very fast – Las Vegas is one of the world's fastest growing cities. Tokyo has experienced enormous growth in the past 50 years with a population of over 13 million, not including the 2.5 million commuters who arrive every day.

Check your understanding

Tested

Fill in case study details for ONE city in the developing world and ONE in the developed world.

	Developing world city	Developed world city
Fact file – size, growth rate, economy		
Causes of growth	1 2 3	1 2 3
Consequences of growth	1 2 3	1 2 3

Knowing the basics

Slums are a frequent result of rapid urban growth. They are very poor quality housing but may be better than some rural housing.

examiner tip

Make sure that you know the difference between economic and social causes and consequences.

How to make living spaces more sustainable

Singapore – a sustainable city?

Singapore is one of the world's best-known cities. It is a city state – that is the city and the country are identical – there is no 'countryside', no rural area, no land other than the 640 km^2 of the city itself in which 4.5 million people live. Almost everything has to be imported; even most of the water comes from Malaysia across the narrow straits. As a result, becoming more sustainable creates particular problems. The government has done a great deal to reach its targets:

- All new urban development has to be self-contained. Offices, factories, shops, services and houses all have to be in easy walking distance of each other.
- Car ownership is discouraged and very expensive. You need to buy a certificate of entitlement that allows you to buy a car before you can purchase one. These certificates cost as much as £5000.
- Singapore invented congestion charging.
- Singapore has one the world's most modern and integrated public transport systems.
- Nearly 60 per cent of waste is recycled with very heavy fines for disobeying the rules. New land is being made at Semakau where waste that cannot be recycled is being used to reclaim land from the sea.
- Waste that has to go to incinerators is used to generate electricity for the city.
- Water is recycled through the NEWater project. Wastewater is treated and used again – many times.
- All new buildings have to conform to the 'Green Mark' scheme involving building design incorporating solar energy and increased use of greenery (on roofs for example).
- Emission controls on vehicles are very tight and heavy industry is restricted to a few areas of the island to improve air quality.

Figure 6 A solar panel in Singapore. An example of the Green Mark scheme in action

What is the potential for 'sustainable cities'?

Revised

Building new cities is not cheap and the plans are affected by economic and political change.

- Eco-towns planned for the UK in the early years of this century were more or less abandoned by the government elected in 2010. The rules were changed making them less 'sustainable' – only 'North West Bicester' remains of the 10 proposed.

- Dongtan, the planned eco-city outside Shanghai in China, has made virtually no progress. Dongtan consists today of 10 wind turbines and no buildings, water taxis, water cleansing plant or energy centres. Construction was to have started in 2006 but nothing has happened yet. The project's co-ordinator has been convicted of corruption and jailed.

- Masdar, the eco-city planned in Abu Dhabi, has been considerably delayed and has had major changes in the plans, for example abandoning self-sufficiency in solar energy. Critics have suggested that if completed the city will become a gated suburb occupied by a rich élite who carry on very unsustainable lifestyles outside the city.

Individuals who live in cities can help make cities more sustainable. As many as 94 per cent of Europeans claim to care about the environment but relatively few make significant changes to their lifestyles.

examiner tip

Questions that ask you to write about how cities can become more sustainable should focus on what planners do.

Individuals can be encouraged to recycle and insulate their homes just as they do in Singapore by grants and advertising campaigns.

examiner tip

Pictures and posters are often used as a resource in exam questions. You will be asked to interpret these.

Knowing the basics

City planners have many opportunities to reduce their city's eco-footprint including transport, water, waste management and building regulations.

Stretch and challenge

It may not be easy for a government to persuade a population to be 'greener' in times of economic difficulty. People may be reluctant to vote for those politicians suggesting policies that might cost more money in the short term.

Exam focus

1   Study Figure 1 on page 22 and the quotes from the survey. Which of the following is seen as a 'major factor' in making France so attractive?   [1]

    A. Its countryside.

    B. Its people.

    C. Its food.

    D. Its variety.

2   State TWO reasons why young people may not find rural life to be ideal.   [2]

3   Identify TWO economic reasons why some living spaces are less attractive to people in work.   [2]

4   Study the material on 'Detroit love' on page 23. Which of the following does the blogger find attractive about present-day Detroit?   [1]

    A. The jobs available.

    B. The education system.

    C. The music.

    D. The health system.

5   Define the term 'rural idyll'.   [2]

6   Outline TWO reasons why young people might be attracted to urban living spaces.   [4]

7   What is meant by the term 'retirement migration'?   [2]

8   Describe TWO possible advantages of living overseas when retired.   [4]

9   Identify TWO pressures on rural areas in developed countries.   [2]

10   Outline ONE possible reason why some rural regions in developed countries have ageing populations.   [2]

11   Which of the following is the main reason for the rapid growth of cities in the developing world?   [1]

    A. Migration from other countries.

    B. A very high birth rate.

    C. Migration from other cities.

    D. Migration from the countryside.

12   Explain ONE reason why very large cities have grown in the developed world.   [2]

13   Define the term 'sustainable city'.   [2]

14   Outline TWO ways in which cities can be made more sustainable.   [4]

15   Suggest ONE reason why it is difficult to make sustainable cities.   [2]

16   Outline TWO ways in which **individuals** can help make cities more sustainable.   [4]

Answers online

Chapter 4 Making a Living
How and why is work changing in different places?

Changing employment at different stages of development

Revised

Employment can be divided into different types:

Employment type	Definition	Example(s)
Primary	Extracting material from the land or sea	Farming, fishing, forestry
Secondary	Manufacturing things	Computers, mobile phones, crisps and chewing gum
Tertiary	Jobs that do not produce a product but provide a service	Teachers, dinner ladies, social workers, care assistants
Quaternary	Jobs based on developing information and selling ideas	Writing computer software, researching biotechnology, creating new knowledge that can be sold

The numbers working in these categories change over time and from place to place. This has been described in the **Clark–Fisher model** (Figure 1).

Figure 1 The Clark–Fisher model of changing employment

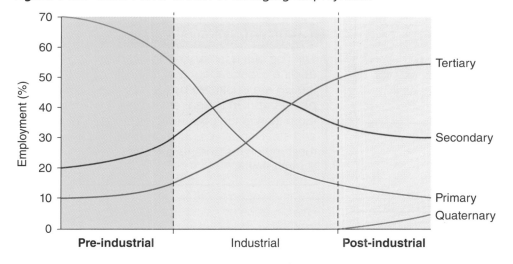

examiner tip

Remember that this is a 'model'. Countries do not 'follow' any pathway automatically; for example Iceland has a highly developed economy yet fishing is the most important sector in that economy.

Pre-industrial societies

Primary industry; mostly farming. A few simple manufacturing industries such as textile and clothing exist plus some metal making. The UK was like this before 1700, a few countries in sub-Saharan Africa today, such as Niger, are still dominated by farming.

Industrial societies

Over time, manufacturing developed (**industrialisation**), especially industries that made goods for people (consumer goods). Primary jobs decline as machinery replaces people. Tertiary jobs develop to provide services in transport, education and other areas.

Post-industrial societies

Many developed nations have lost jobs in manufacturing as these have moved to emerging developing nations. Primary industry has continued to decline while tertiary activities have grown and the quaternary sector has developed.

Contrasting countries

Mexico – an industrialising country	The UK – a de-industrialising country
Fact file **GDP** per capita = $15,000 Size of economy = thirteenth largest in the world Primary 18%, secondary 24%, tertiary and quaternary 58%	**Fact file** **GDP per capita** = $34,000 Size of economy = sixth largest in the world Primary 2%, secondary 10%, tertiary and quaternary 88%

- Mexico is a large economy that has experienced many changes. Only 50 years ago over 50 per cent of its population worked in farming, mostly as peasants farming land which they didn't own
- Agriculture is still important but it is increasingly carried out on very large estates growing crops for export
- Its very rich northern neighbour (the USA) has moved a lot of factories into Mexico to take advantage of the cheaper labour and Mexican companies have grown to supply an increasing home market and for export
- As wealth has grown so have tertiary activities such as jobs in shops and tourism, which the government is encouraging
- Mexico has lost some of its foreign companies as they have moved to even cheaper labour locations such as China and Bangladesh

- The UK was a pioneer country in the eighteenth and nineteenth centuries – the first to industrialise. By the early part of the twentieth century as many as 40 per cent of workers were employed in the secondary sector
- Mining remained an important part of the primary sector as late as the early twentieth century – there were a million miners in 1911
- Today, manufacturing has declined because of mechanisation replacing workers with machines and robots, as well as the movement of industries abroad
- Successive governments have also had a role to play with an emphasis on finance and business services, which have been seen as the way forward, along with quaternary activities in information technology and research
- Farming still dominates the landscape but employs very few people

Knowing the basics

Manufacturing industry has moved to cheaper labour locations to reduce costs for the companies. This brings jobs but, as in Mexico, they may not last.

Stretch and challenge

The rise of the tertiary sector in the UK and the decline of secondary and primary industry in the UK are illustrated by the fact that 70,000 people work in Indian restaurants in the UK; more than in the coal industry, shipbuilding and steel industries put together. Ironically most Indian restaurants are owned by Bangladeshis.

examiner tip

Remember that no two developing or developed countries have the same employment structure. For example, nearly 25 per cent of Germany's GDP comes from manufacturing industries.

The USA in retreat?

- The USA has lost approximately 42,400 factories since 2001; that represents 5.5 million jobs.
- Dell Inc., one of the world's largest computer manufacturers, plans to expand its operations in China with an investment of over $100 billion. The company closed its last large factory in the USA with the loss of 900 jobs.
- In 2008, global mobile phones sales reached 1.2 billion. Not any of these handsets were manufactured in the USA.
- Some people say that if the US trade deficit with China increases at its current rate, the US economy will lose over half a million jobs a year. China owns $1.5 trillion of American debt.

The impact of industrialisation on an industrialising country

Revised

Mexico

- A large number of informal jobs (30 per cent of all jobs) but no stability in these.
- The jobs being created are not of the highest quality.
- 'I'd rather find something more stable, but at my age it's not so easy,' said Orozco, aged 59, a former police officer.
- Mexico does not offer jobless benefits.
- The **informal economy** is important everywhere. These jobs are not 'official' with little or no tax paid and no records kept.
- Large, formal enterprises offer stability and benefits that can give security and increase spending.
- Rural to urban migration has brought over 1000 migrants a day to Mexico City because there is no work in the countryside and little hope of getting any secure employment.
- Agriculture is dominated by large agribusiness, reflecting this very uneven society where 85 per cent of the national wealth is concentrated in a few families.
- Mexican business magnate Carlos Slim is the richest man in the world and has a personal fortune equal to about five per cent of the whole country's GDP.

Knowing the basics

It is obvious that Mexico City has grown enormously at an accelerated rate.

So why has the informal economy grown?

- Not enough 'formal' jobs.
- Large numbers of new immigrants.
- Need to survive by finding something to do – selling, trading and so on.
- Lack of regulations.

Why have rural economies had to diversify?

The changing face of rural communities in the UK

- There are about 300,000 farms with an average size of around 57 hectares.
- Farms are getting bigger – farms larger than 100 hectares make up over 65 per cent of the agricultural area.
- Today British farming employs less than 500,000 people; 200,000 of these jobs are part-time.
- There are four million jobs in the food processing and related industries.
- Farmers are responsible for looking after around 75 per cent of the UK's surface area and for maintaining the countryside.
- Agriculture contributes 0.6 per cent of the UK's GDP.

Prince warns 'Countryside could become scrubland and ghost villages'

The Prince of Wales thinks that upland areas such as the Lake District, Exmoor and the Yorkshire Dales will become nothing more than 'extreme adventure playgrounds' for people to go hang-gliding or paraponting.

Prince Charles would like consumers to buy British produce and contribute towards a new fund, the Prince's Countryside Fund, he has set up to support people in remote rural areas. The fund will give money to charities in these areas.

Villages have declined all over the world. At one time rural settlements were largely self-sufficient with food grown to feed the family and extras paid for by selling a cash crop in the local market – a subsistence economy. These 'peasant' economies have not survived in Europe and people have left the countryside in large numbers.

The same processes of change are now obvious in many developing countries. The best land in many poor countries is controlled by a small wealthy class who farm commercially – often inedible crops such as palm oil or cotton for export. Peasants lose their land and so too their chances of survival – they have to travel to cities in the hope of better prospects.

Rural diversification is an attempt to provide a wider range of income and employment in the countryside. The core reasons are:

- The decline in the importance of agriculture in most developed countries.
- Fewer farms with fewer full-time jobs mean fewer children in school, fewer people to use local shops.
- More people, especially young people, are leaving for the city.
- Farming is uncertain – even in good times the risks of a bad harvest or disease make it a high-risk business.
- In the past farming was subsidised, but not any longer.

Knowing the basics

Farming is in decline: this is the basic cause of seeking diversification.

Stretch and challenge

Rural jobs are often poorly paid and sometimes part-time and/or temporary.

Keeping people in the countryside

- Jobs, and preferably well-paid jobs, better transport facilities and services are top of the wish list for most rural communities in the developed world. This is hardly an issue in rural areas close to major cities, but the more distant the city, the more remote the area becomes and the greater the need to address the communication problem.
- **Broadband connectivity** and good mobile networks would help and potentially allow new businesses to develop.
- Tourism obviously plays a key role here, but not always without some costs as well.

How can the environmental impacts of changing work be managed more sustainably?

The impact of de-industrialisation and employment change on the environment – the developed world

- Developed societies tend to have fewer jobs in the manufacturing industry (**de-industrialisation**) – the secondary sector as the Clark–Fisher model describes it – but to call these societies post-industrial is a bit misleading because some sectors have become much more industrial (see the material on feedlots on page 36).

- De-industrialisation can also have negative effects because abandoned buildings and waste materials can cause problems. However, there can be positive effects with improved air and water quality and a 'greening' of a city.

- Changes also take place elsewhere and these can directly and indirectly have huge impacts on the environment. By most measures the USA is the most advanced developed society in the world and it provides many good examples of these changes.

De-industrialising Detroit – one million and shrinking

- Detroit is getting smaller; once a city of 2.5 million people and the most important industrial city in the USA, it now has a population of around one million and its industries have largely gone.
- Impacts include:
  - Abandoned factories.
  - Toxic waste draining into groundwater.
  - Damage to wildlife from industrial waste.
- But also good things:
  - The greening of the city as nature takes back the abandoned residential and industrial areas.
  - Urban farms – open space turned over to agriculture.
  - Water and air pollution improving – fish have returned to the Detroit river after over 100 years of it being almost lifeless.

> **examiner tip**
> Remember that impacts can be **positive** as well as **negative**.

> **Stretch and challenge**
> The industries that used to pollute Detroit have moved outside the city or sometimes abroad. Some of this production takes place in Mexico City.

Figure 2 Abandoned residential and industrial areas in Detroit have resulted in the greening of the city

Changing agriculture – feedlot America

Small farms are disappearing and agribusiness is growing. A good example is the growth of factories farming beef and pork on huge feedlots.

The environmental impacts of feedlots are often very negative:

- Ten people could be fed with the grain that is used to feed a cow.
- It takes 20,000–40,000 litres of water to produce 1 kg of beef.
- Up to 100,000 animals are herded together on huge feedlots.
- Feedlots are crowded, filthy, stinking places with open sewers, unpaved roads and choking air.
- The animals are fed huge amounts of antibiotics which then find their way into the water system.
- In a feedlot with 37,000 cows, 25 tonnes of corn are consumed every hour. (Corn makes the animals fatten up faster than feeding them with their natural diet of grass.)
- Oil is used to produce corn: 3500 litres of oil for each hectare. A factory-raised cow is not so much a 'solar-powered' grazing animal but a 'fossil fuel' machine.
- Livestock now produces 130 times the amount of waste that people do. This waste is untreated and unsanitary, poisoning rivers, killing fish and getting into human drinking water.
- 65 per cent of California's population is threatened by polluted drinking water.
- Even the oceans are polluted: 20,000 km^2 of the Gulf of Mexico are a dead zone.
- And on top of all this, there is the fuel used to transport the livestock and the meat around the country.

Supermarkets on the march

Post-industrial societies have large retail sectors often dominated by supermarket chains:

- Most people drive to supermarkets.
- Supermarkets offer a wide range of goods often sourced overseas so with large carbon footprints.
- New supermarkets have often been built on **greenfield sites** with a loss of habitat and farmland.

The impact of industrialisation and employment change on the environment – the developing world

Revised ☐

- The growth of the manufacturing industry is usually accompanied by environmental problems because making things is often quite a messy business.
- De-industrialisation in the developed world has occurred partly because industrialisation has taken place in the developing world – we (the developed world) have 'exported' our dirty industries.
- Other changes have also had an impact on the environment, not least the changes in the countryside in countries such as India, China, Nigeria and Mexico, which have driven people into cities.

Industrialising Mexico City – 20 million and growing

- Causes of air pollution are:
  - factories – fewer now than in the 1970s and 1980s
  - power stations
  - cars and lorries – there are over 10 million vehicles in Mexico City
  - domestic heating.
- The situation is made worse because:
  - The city is surrounded by mountains so any air pollution is trapped.
  - It is situated at over 2000 metres above sea level, so oxygen is thinner – this makes pollution worse.
  - It has a subtropical climate with clear skies.
  - Poor quality of pollution controls.
  - Old vehicles, badly maintained, and not designed for high altitudes.
- Other environmental impacts include:
  - Lack of water – underground aquifers are not being topped up so the ground is sinking.
  - 10,000 tonnes of rubbish are collected every day – but 1000 tonnes are not collected and just accumulate.
  - Quality of water is poor with chemical pollution from garbage and industrial waste.

Changing agriculture – the march of agribusiness

- Mexico's agribusiness uses more fertilisers and other chemicals, costing $36 billion per year in pollution.
- Poor rural farmers are expanding into more marginal land, resulting in deforestation at a rate of 630,000 hectares per year.
- Mexico loses its forest at a rate of about 0.9 per cent every year due to agricultural and industrial expansion.
- Mexico has the fourth largest mangrove area in the world, covering approximately one million hectares. Much of it is under threat from coastal development and tourism.
- In 2001, 64 of the nation's mammal species and 36 bird species were endangered.

examiner tip

As countries develop, the environment is not usually high on the agenda.

Stretch and challenge

The quality of the environment is much better in the rich, suburban areas occupied by the better off.

How to regenerate brownfield sites

Revised ☐

- **Brownfield sites** are urban areas that have already been developed and are now available for redevelopment as part of **urban regeneration**.
- Most post-industrial cities have areas once occupied by factories or housing that grew up around those factories.
- In 2000 one of the largest concentrations of brownfield sites in Europe was in east London; an area that was once a major centre of British industry.
- What will be left after London's 2012 Olympics will be the regeneration of one of the most deprived parts of the country with a very large number of brownfield sites.
- The problems with such projects are:
  - What are the present benefits for local people in terms of jobs and the environment?
  - Are the developments sustainable? Will the benefits be obvious after the games have finished?
  - Will the area change so much that the current population is unable to afford to stay there? Or is it just expensive gentrification?

11,000 new houses have been built within the Olympic Park, around a third of which were planned as affordable homes. Regeneration of the surrounding area – one of the most deprived in Britain – is a core goal.

The two biggest housing problems in the area are children living in high-rise flats and overcrowding. Much of the new housing will not meet these families' needs and is not available to them. Most of the new houses are for sale on the open market and those labelled as affordable housing are for sale through shared ownership schemes.

Research has indicated that poorer residents could only enter owner-occupation if house prices were very low. This is not the case and therefore people looking for better housing will have to look to the small number of homes for social renting.

Housing waiting lists in the Olympic's London boroughs

Newham: 28,649
Tower Hamlets: 19,681
Waltham Forest: 14,341
Hackney: 11,461
Greenwich: 7,902
Source: Adapted from BBC News website (6 December 2010).

Figure 3 An example of brownfield site redevelopment – the 2012 Olympic Park

Stretch and challenge

Almost all large projects have both winners and losers. Left to themselves large companies will try to make as large a profit as they can. It is up to government and planners to insist that profit is not the only motive.

What is the 'green economy' and how will it grow?

The idea that how we travel, the workplaces we develop and the homes we live in should become more sustainable has led to the growth of many jobs that did not exist 20 years ago.

- Making things more sustainable has led to a '**green economy**'.
- New jobs have been made or there has been a change of emphasis in the daily routine of existing jobs.
- Some of the reasons for the growth of the green economy are listed in the table below.

Cause/pressure	Job(s)	Comment
The problem of non-renewable resources – especially oil	Research, design and service jobs in developing new energy sources	Some of the most active companies in this field are oil companies who know that the era of cheap oil cannot last forever Chevron spends £300 million a year on research with its subsidiary Chevron Energy Solutions. It made $19 billion profit in 2010 (mostly from oil)
The problem of climate change	There are many jobs involved in developing ways of using energy more efficiently and reducing carbon dioxide emissions, including designing and constructing better buildings	New building materials are being used or very old ones are being used in new ways. Straw has been revived as a building material. Recycled materials such as glass are also used, for example, in making worktops and flooring materials
Water and waste issues	Water shortages and the difficulty of disposing of waste are major problems especially in cities. New companies have developed and existing companies have changed direction	In dry areas of the USA such as Nevada or Arizona the enormous use of water to keep lawns green in arid climates is obviously non-sustainable. A new type of landscape management job has come about, known as 'xeriscaping' or 'xerogardening', with no grass and drought-resistant plants
Responding to changing consumer demand	Green consumerism has provided opportunities for producers to adapt their existing products or develop new ones that are in demand. Jobs can be generated in farming and other rural activities	Organic farming isn't sustainable just because it is organic but if it reduces the use of fertilisers, pesticides and herbicides it is likely to be more sustainable than intensive modern methods Farmers' markets have become popular in recent years in the UK, allowing local producers to find local customers

The potential for growth

Governments can encourage the green economy with grants and loans. However, these incentives can be taken away in times of economic difficulty. This happened in 2011 when the Spanish government withdrew grants for installing solar panels.

Exam focus

1 Which of the following is a job in the tertiary sector? [1]

  A. Working on a fishing trawler.

  B. Working in a fast-food restaurant.

  C. Working on a farm.

  D. Working in a car factory.

2 Study Figure 1 on page 31. Describe the changes in secondary employment. [3]

3 Which of the following best defines de-industrialisation? [1]

  A. The loss of jobs in farming.

  B. The movement of firms to more rural locations in a country.

  C. The decline of manufacturing jobs.

  D. An increase in jobs in the secondary sector.

4 Identify TWO differences between industrialising and de-industrialising countries. [2]

5 Define the term 'informal economy'. [2]

6 Outline TWO reasons why the informal economy is important in developing countries. [4]

7 Which of the following is an example of rural diversification? [1]

  A. Creating urban farms to help feed the population.

  B. The growth of deserts in developing countries.

  C. Creating new types of employment in the countryside.

  D. Encouraging the growth of second home ownership.

8 Suggest TWO reasons why villages and rural areas might lose population. [2]

9 Study Figure 2 on page 35. Identify TWO pieces of evidence that Detroit is suffering employment loss. [2]

10 Describe TWO ways in which de-industrialisation can affect the environment. [4]

11 Outline ONE reason why industrialisation is likely to damage the environment. [2]

12 Identify TWO sources of air pollution in cities in the developing world. [2]

13 Which of the following is the best definition of a brownfield site? [1]

  A. A field that has yet to be planted.

  B. An area in a city that should be developed.

  C. An agricultural area that might be developed for housing.

  D. An area in a city that was once built on and can now be redeveloped.

14 Read the material on the Olympic Park on page 38. Describe TWO problems in providing housing for poorer residents. [4]

15 Define the term 'green economy'. [2]

16 Describe the characteristics of ONE job within the green economy. [3]

Answers online

Section B Small-scale People and the Planet
Chapter 5 Changing Cities
What are the environmental issues facing cities?

The impact of cities

- **Ecological footprints (eco-footprints)** vary from place to place. They measure the amount of land required to support a population – to make comparison easier it is usually expressed 'per capita' (that is to say per individual person).

- When looked at this way, people who live in cities are usually slightly lower users than national averages. London's ecological footprint is 4.54 global hectares (gha) per person (2006). This is slightly lower than the UK average of 4.64 gha per person.

- Although London's footprint is lower than the UK average, the high consumption of resources means it is about twice the size of the global average footprint of 2.6 gha per person. When divided equally between the world's population, it is 2.5 times bigger than the bio-capacity of the land (1.8 gha per person). Bio-capacity is the area of land available to supply natural resources.

- Half of the world's population lives in large cities and many of them are growing rapidly. So the total ecological footprint of large cities is very high; for example London's is over 34 million hectares. This is 200 times the area of the city.

Figure 1 Ecological footprint of London

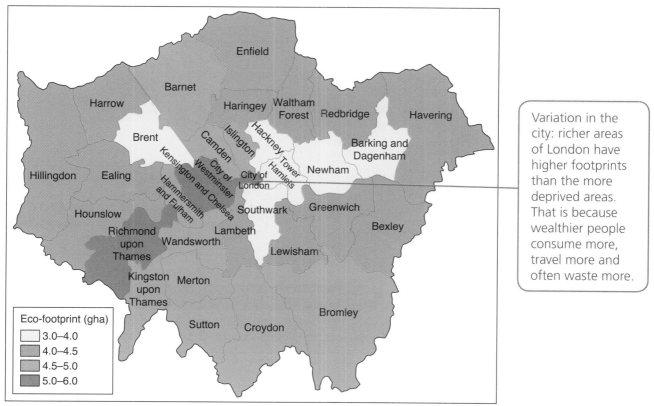

Variation in the city: richer areas of London have higher footprints than the more deprived areas. That is because wealthier people consume more, travel more and often waste more.

Eco-footprint (gha)
- 3.0–4.0
- 4.0–4.5
- 4.5–5.0
- 5.0–6.0

- Cities are bound to have relatively high eco-footprints because they cannot support themselves. Most cities grew up as markets where specialist trades developed selling these products in exchange for food.
- The lowest footprints on the planet are to be found in very poor societies where almost everything needed is produced by the household. We call this a subsistence society.
- Although large footprints may not mean that something has gone wrong, the fact remains that cities vary hugely in their footprints and they can almost always be reduced. It is obviously a good thing to turn cities into more **eco-friendly organisms**.
- Low-density cities such as Los Angeles or Atlanta will have higher footprints than high-density cities such as Barcelona because of the fuel used just to get around.

Knowing the basics

If cities grew more food then their footprints would be reduced.

Stretch and challenge

- Large cities have large footprints because of their size but average footprints may be higher in some smaller cities. Las Vegas is an example.
- Economic recession would inevitably reduce footprints – if you never have another holiday that too would reduce your footprint.

Tested ☐

Check your understanding

State TWO reasons why a city's average footprint might increase.

Why do our footprints vary?

Revised ☐

Footprints are measured by investigating how much land is required to provide for the needs listed below. Of course, it isn't a real piece of land that you can visit, but just an idea of how much space would be needed to provide for all your needs. These needs include the following:

- **Food** – areas associated with food production.
- **Shelter** – energy used in providing buildings.
- **Mobility** – fuel and land used for transport.
- **Goods** – consumption associated with making things.
- **Services** – disposing of waste, entertainment, health services.

examiner tip

Make sure that you do not confuse the average footprint of people in a city with the total footprint of that city.

Knowing the basics

Poor people have small eco-footprints.

Stretch and challenge

It is a lot easier for wealthy people to reduce their footprints because they often consume more and waste more.

Tested ☐

Check your understanding

Look at Figure 2 on page 43. State TWO reasons why car owners have a higher footprint than cyclists.

Figure 2 How individuals have very different footprints

Who, where?	Food	Shelter	Mobility	Goods	Services	Total
Richard – an IT consultant Atlanta – a city in the USA	Richard eats out frequently but also buys food at the supermarket – much of this food is imported	Richard has a large detached house in Marietta on the outskirts of Atlanta – it is well insulated and has a state-of-art air-conditioning system. He also has a swimming pool	He drives to work in a large air-conditioned car – 80 km a day on average – he takes summer holidays in Florida and goes to Colorado for skiing	Richard owns two cars and a large motorbike – he has a wide range of high-tech electronic appliances in his house	He recycles but produces a lot of waste. He visits a health club and plays golf at the local course	15 gha (Atlanta average 9.6 gha). Richard is a wealthy individual in a wealthy country. He has a typically high eco-footprint and although he cares about the environment he enjoys his lifestyle
Doris – a farmer A small town in Vermont – one of the most rural parts of the USA	Local shops have shut down in recent years – she has to drive 45 km to the nearest supermarket	Doris lives in a draughty old farmhouse 15 km from the local town. She has an inefficient air-conditioning system and uses large wood-burning stoves in the winter	Doris drives an old gas-guzzling pick-up truck. She drives 30 km a day on the school run but visits her mother every weekend – a round trip of 200 km. She occasionally visits friends in New York	Doris has a lot of machinery and uses a great deal of oil-based products on the farm. She has a modern kitchen and a wide range of electronic equipment	Doris recycles and is careful about what she buys, avoiding packaged goods, but she throws away about 20 per cent of all purchased food unused	13 gha (Vermont average 8.5 gha). The problem for Doris and many others is the long distances that she has to travel in her rural area. Her supermarket stocks largely imported goods. Rural living may seem greener but it often isn't
Aditi – an IT worker Mumbai – a city in India	Aditi eats at home with her family. The diet is simple and like most Indian cities the food is largely from the surrounding region – she eats out occasionally with friends	Aditi rents an apartment with her parents. She hopes to move out soon to a new apartment in an integrated suburb in Goregaon – a new western suburb	Aditi catches a train to work and walks 3 km every day to and from the stations. Once a year she visits her grandparents 150 km away in Maharashtra. She has never had a holiday	Aditi has a bicycle and one day hopes to own a cheap car – maybe a Tata Nano. She has a mobile phone and a small TV that she shares with her parents. She hopes to buy an iPhone soon	Aditi lives in a very active community – there is a lively theatre and cinema club over the street – she dances as a hobby with two friends in a local community centre	1.4 gha (Mumbai average 0.8 gha). Most of Mumbai's population is much poorer than Aditi and live in very poor conditions. As a member of India's growing middle class it is likely that her eco-footprint will rise in years to come
Rahul – a farmer Maharashtra – a state in India	Rahul and his family grow almost all that they eat on their 1.5 ha – a diet based on millet and a few vegetables. Cash crops are sold locally for extras	The house is rented from the same landlord as the farm. Cooking is by wood or cow dung and there are no modern appliances or utilities. Water has be carried from the local well	The farm is next to the house with one piece of land 1 km away by the river. Journeys beyond the village are rare – one or two visits to family in local villages and an annual visit to a local holy site	The family have an old bike that they share. They have never visited a supermarket and apart from a few simple cooking utensils they own very little	The family produce little waste and use some of that on the land! They occasionally watch the communal television in the village	0.5 gha (Maharashtra average 0.9 gha). The most important reason for very low eco-footprints is poverty. Raising people out of poverty means increasing their consumption, which will raise their eco-footprint

How do cities develop and grow?

- Cities are centres of wealth creation. They are also centres of control where governments and the rich and powerful have lived.
- In ancient Rome, the ruling class got their wealth from their large country estates worked by slaves but they lived in the city. In modern Brazil, wealthy landowners still tend to live in the cities.
- In the nineteenth century, new types of cities emerged as the industrial revolution drew people together to work in factories. This process, known as industrialisation, began in Europe. In modern Asia and Africa, cities have grown rapidly in recent years driven partly by industrialisation but also by changes in the countryside.
- Europe industrialised early. London was the first city with a population of one million. London's growth was based around its status as a capital of an empire and a major centre for industry.
- Asian cities are often very ancient, but many like Mumbai and Shanghai have grown very rapidly in the past 20 or 30 years as India and China have industrialised.

Check your understanding

State TWO reasons why post-industrial cities have lower footprints than industrial cities.

London

Figure 3 London's eco-footprint compared with other cities

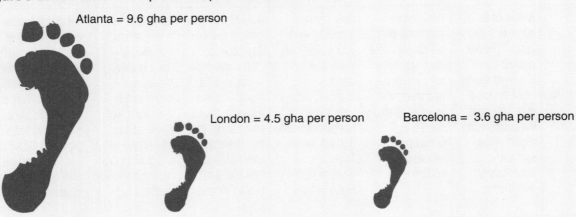

Atlanta = 9.6 gha per person

London = 4.5 gha per person

Barcelona = 3.6 gha per person

- London's eco-footprint has changed as the city has changed.
- The UK has de-industrialised and the heavy industries that were once a feature of areas such as the Docklands and the East End have gone.
- As industry has been replaced by offices and less polluting activities, carbon dioxide emissions are quite low compared to other post-industrial cities.
- Remember that the goods that were once made in the city are now made elsewhere and are often imported, so savings made on one part of footprint will be set against the costs of importing goods.
- Cities that industrialised quite early are usually densely populated and have good public transport systems – this reduces air pollution and carbon dioxide from transportation.
- But again it is worth remembering that waste is also exported. A third of London's old computers end up back in China where many of them were made.
- So one city might get 'cleaner' and 'greener' while other cities' eco-footprints get larger.

What 7.5 million Londoners consume in a year
- 150,000 gigawatt-hours of energy – that is equivalent to 13 million tonnes of oil.
- 50 million tonnes of materials.
- Seven million tonnes of food.
- Nearly 900 billion litres of water.

How far Londoners travel
- 64 billion kilometres – 70 per cent by car.

What Londoners throw away
- 26 million tonnes of rubbish, of which 3.5 million tonnes is from households and the rest from construction and industry.

Stretch and challenge
Tourists to London are estimated to add another 0.32 gha to every Londoner's footprint.

The impact of cities on their surrounding regions
Revised

Cities have an impact on their surrounding regions in a number of ways:

- Singapore, a city state, affects Malaysia not just because of the movement of people but because Malaysia sells water to Singapore.
- Other cities are rather like islands in that the surrounding region is more or less deserted – this is the case with Las Vegas. This obviously makes issues regarding **landfill** and sewage disposal much simpler than when the surrounding area is densely populated as with London or New York.
- For many years the disposal of waste for coastal cities posed very few problems because most of it was simply washed into the river. The River Thames was known for the 'Great Stink' of the 1850s, and even in the 1950s it was pretty much a lifeless river.

Check your understanding
Tested

Fill in the case study details below of your chosen city:

Chosen city ....
Impact 1
Impact 2
Impact 3

Knowing the basics
Growing cities have an impact most directly on surrounding rural areas by turning them into urban areas.

Stretch and challenge
There are potential positives from urban growth – demand for goods may raise incomes and new activities for urban dwellers allow farms to diversify.

How far can these issues be resolved sustainably?

How cities are reducing their eco-footprints

Revised ☐

For cities to reduce their eco-footprints they need:

- to become more compact, not unlike Paris but with bicycles and rickshaws rather than cars
- buildings limited to less than six storeys
- plenty of open spaces
- dense public transport networks
- food markets where the food for sale is from local producers – the food would be less energy intensive and possibly fresher and more interesting
- systems in place allowing people to recycle and save energy at home.

Portland, Oregon, USA

Figure 4 Portland: a sustainable city?

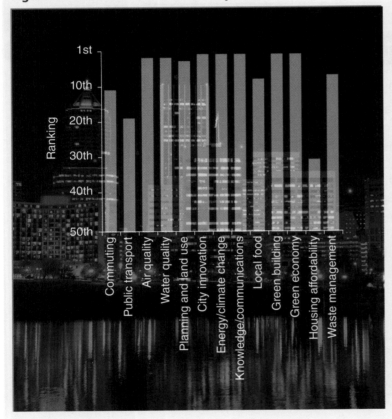

Portland has regularly come top of American league tables for sustainable cities. It achieves this through:

- An urban planning system that has prevented urban sprawl leading to a denser and largely pedestrian-friendly city centre.
- Support for the development of green retailing – plastic bags are banned in large supermarkets.
- The Green Investment Fund (GIF) is a five-year programme to support innovative green building projects within the city.
- The development of a tramway system as part of an integrated transport network including support for bikes.
- Grants for planting; the city government offers a rebate of up to $40 ($50 for native species) for trees planted on people's property.

Knowing the basics

Urban sprawl makes journeys longer and so wastes more energy.

examiner tip

In general, try not to use extreme terms likes 'richest' or 'worst'. It is better to use comparative words such as 'richer' and 'worse'.

Stretch and challenge

Cities need to be planned with mixed land uses so that most services can be accessed on foot or by bike.

- Most cities have local governments with quite a lot of power to make their cities more sustainable.
- City planners do not have to be especially committed to sustainable development to see that they need to do something about transport systems. As cities change and grow, the problems of moving people about grow with them.
- In Beijing, China, there are about 1500 new cars registered every day. Traffic congestion is growing rapidly with average bus speeds of only 10 km/hour because of it.
- Cities with inefficient transport systems will be economically less efficient and less attractive, causing more problems in the future.

City planners have a number of possible strategies to develop **sustainable transport** alternatives – some much more radical than others.

Strategy	Aim	Example(s)	Comment
Greenbelt policies These are planning restrictions on the outward growth of the city – new building of any sort in these areas is forbidden	To prevent urban sprawl. This increases the density of development within the urban area and makes it cheaper to provide public transport	London was the first major city to have a greenbelt. Most US cities do not have them and neither do cities in countries where the planning system is weak	Stopping cities from developing outwards might create 'leap-frogging', with new developments taking place outside the greenbelt making commuting journeys longer
Self-contained urban development Urban development that is self-contained has offices, retail and residential all close together in the same area	To prevent unnecessary use of transport. If people have jobs and all basic facilities in walking distance of where they live they use their transport less often	Singapore's Urban Redevelopment Authority has considerable power and all new developments have been self-contained	In the past planners preferred to keep different land uses apart. This 'neighbourhood' principle increases the need to travel
Integrated transport systems An integrated system is one where the rail, bus and even taxi systems are planned to work together. So as people arrive at stations there are buses to take them from station to work or home. One ticket covers all journeys	To prevent the unnecessary use of cars. In developed cities many inhabitants own cars. Cars are flexible and not limited by timetables or fixed routes. Persuading car owners to leave cars at home is much easier if the alternative methods of moving about are flexible too	Barcelona and Singapore both have integrated systems. They both have very strong local governments and a population who are committed to the principles of public transport. Cities such as Atlanta and Las Vegas have very limited public transport and relatively weak governance	Public transport is often provided by private companies who are interested in making a profit and may not be too concerned about the next stage of a commuter's journey. It will often need the city planners to make sure that the co-ordination takes place
Encouraging bicycles Bicycles are a sustainable form of transport with other benefits for the health of the population in improving both air quality and the physical fitness of users	To increase the use of non-polluting bikes. This can be done by building bike lanes and, more radically, providing bicycles for people to rent in the city	Paris, Toulouse, Barcelona and Portland are four examples among many. London has also introduced a scheme with over 5000 bikes and 400 docking stations where bikes can be picked up and left	These schemes have been successful although they usually need a subsidy from the taxpayer to make them affordable. The London system costs £45 a year for users with a rental charge on top after a free 30 minutes
Congestion charging A tax on vehicles entering the city	To keep cars out of city centres by making it expensive. This can be achieved in a number of ways but modern technology has helped these systems become more effective without slowing traffic flows	Singapore was the pioneer and now has an electronic road pricing system by which variable charges are applied and automatically taken from users' bank accounts according to usage	Some cities such as Manchester have rejected congestion charging and US cities where reliance on the car is very high have been very slow to adopt it
Car-sharing or rationing schemes	As above – to keep cars out of city centres. This can be achieved by encouraging car-sharing, restricting access by having lanes on roads that can only be used by high-occupancy vehicles (HOVs)	Many US cities such as Los Angeles have HOV-only lanes on their urban motorways	Some US cities have also introduced HOT lanes – a variation on the HOV theme that allows drivers to pay a toll to use them even when on their own
Bus lanes, park-and-ride schemes Cars can be left on the edge of cities and people are then transported into the city by bus	As above – to keep cars out of city centres. By making it easier for people to travel into the city by bus and faster by increasing average speed of bus travel. There are also benefits for air quality	Park and ride schemes have been popular in the UK since the 1960s. Oxford was one of the first and now has five car parks on the edge of the city	It is not clear how successful they have been in reducing congestion and some schemes lack flexibility – for example the scheme in Bath does not operate on Sundays and the distribution of the sites does not suit all visitors

Check your understanding `Tested`

What is congestion charging?

How can green consumerism help?

- **Green consumerism** refers to **recycling**, purchasing and use of eco-friendly products that minimise damage to the environment.
- It is not restricted to cities but can help cities reduce their eco-footprints.
- Once again local governments can have quite an influence on this, although not with the same 'control' as they have with transport.

Strategy	Aim	Examples	What can governments do?
Recycling Consumers separate different types of waste and either take it to centres or have it collected at the kerbside	To save resources and to save money. There is an indirect impact on fossil-fuel use and greenhouse gas production as well	In the UK, recycling of household waste has risen from 27.3 per cent in 2000 to 44.8 per cent in 2008. For some materials such as glass and paper, nearly all is now recycled	Local government has to set up the systems for collection, but most of the processing is carried out by private companies
Food purchasing 1 – organic and fair trade produce An increasing demand for organically produced food and fair trade products	To encourage food and fibre production without using as many non-renewable resources or producing as much waste. This has become linked in some cases with fair trade schemes which give a higher proportion of the sales price to the original producer	There has been a well-supported campaign for fair trade coffee, not least from Ethiopian co-operatives selling the Oromia region's organic coffee. This was popularised in the film *Black Gold*	Not much – governments can promote organic produce in their own region or country
Food purchasing 2 – farmers' markets Markets set up that sell local produce, so reducing 'food miles'	To encourage local producers. This decreases the amount of energy used in transporting food – the 'food miles' figure goes down	There are over 500 farmers' markets in the UK, 250 of them officially arranged. London has several although some of them are not really local	Local government agreement is needed to hold a market. Subsidies might be found and advertising provided
Urban farms Food production in cities both private and commercial	To encourage cities to become more self-sufficient. This will reduce their eco-footprints because less food will need to be imported	No-one knows exactly how many urban farms there are in London but a full meal including wine can now be sourced from within the M25 motorway area. An example is the Giggly Pig Company, which sells pork products throughout London	London and other cities have encouraged urban farms through planning. In the forefront are declining cites such as Detroit, but London has 'London Food', intended to improve sustainability
Energy-saving strategies A wide range of methods that will reduce energy consumption at home, in the workplace and in the wider urban environment	To reduce energy consumption by encouraging both public and private users to replace inefficient energy systems with more efficient and sustainable ones as well as reducing demand for energy	About 55,000 homes in London are to get a free energy efficiency assessment which could lead to reductions in bills. The RE:NEW scheme, includes low-energy light bulbs and radiator panels, being installed for free	Local and national governments can fund and advertise these schemes

Knowing the basics

Governments can encourage green consumerism with positive policies or even by forcing people with laws.

The potential for green consumerism in your local area

Green consumerism is not easy to measure because much of it is unrecorded and private. You could draw up a checklist to keep a watch on the progress being made towards a more sustainable future. Take a look at the following example of local monitoring written before the 2012 Olympics:

The 2012 London Olympic sponsors such as McDonald's and Coca-Cola will serve 20 per cent of all food and drink at the Olympic venues. At the moment it is not clear how sustainable their food and drink supply is.

McDonald's has proposed building a huge restaurant on the Olympic site. Some people have criticised the food giant's ingredients sourcing policy, specifically that its products are not Fairtrade. However, the company states, for example, that coffee is sourced from Rainforest Alliance Certified farms and milk from is obtained from British farms recognised under farm assurance schemes.

Regions which have reduced their eco-footprints

- Flanders, Belgium – variable charging for collection of household waste has led to 73 per cent recycling rates.
- Kirklees, UK – carbon budgeting has saved the council over £1 million.
- Oslo, Norway – bio-methane produced from sewage is used to power public transport, saving €0.40 per litre of fuel.
- Southampton, UK – a district heating scheme powered by geothermal energy which is 85 per cent efficient.
- Kalundborg Eco-Industrial Park, Denmark – a power plant linked to local homes and businesses.

Knowing the basics

There are many organisations that promote fair trade but sometimes the messages are complex, especially when the product is made in China.

examiner tip

Remember that in this section it is important to distinguish between what governments can do and what individuals do.

Check your understanding

1 Define the term 'green consumerism'.
2 State TWO ways in which your local area is trying to reduce its eco-footprint.

Exam focus

1 Study Figure 1 on page 41. Describe the variations in London's eco-footprint. [2]

2 Suggest ONE possible reason why living in low-density cities might be more expensive than living in a high-density city. [4]

3 Outline TWO ways in which individuals can reduce their eco-footprints. [4]

4 Suggest ONE reason why developing countries have low eco-footprints. [2]

5 Explain TWO ways in which post-industrial cities have reduced their eco-footprints. [4]

6 Study the case study on page 44. Identify TWO 'dimensions' in which London performs better than most other cities. [2]

7 Identify TWO ways in which cities in developed countries can reduce their eco-footprints. [2]

8 Outline ONE way in which resources used by a large city affects other parts of the country. [2]

9 Study the case study on page 46. Identify the TWO areas in which Portland does particularly well in achieving sustainability. [2]

10 Using a named example, explain how cities can reduce their eco-footprints. [6]

11 Identify ONE characteristic of a sustainable transport system. [2]

12 For a named city, explain how it has made its transport system more sustainable. [6]

13 Outline ONE way in which green consumerism can help the environment. [2]

14 Describe TWO ways in energy saving can be achieved by consumers. [4]

15 State TWO ways in which your local area promotes green consumerism. [2]

16 Explain how local areas can reduce their carbon footprints. [4]

Answers online

Chapter 6 Changing Countryside
What are the issues facing rural areas?

Revised

The issues facing rural areas under pressure in developed countries

- **Rural poverty** in the sense of lacking the basics of life is very rare in the developed world.
- **Relative poverty** and **deprivation** are not. So rural areas in developed countries face different problems.

Knowing the basics

Rural areas are highly varied. Remote rural areas are still dominated by farming and other primary activities. Those nearer cities are rather like suburbs with more open space.

Stretch and challenge

In the developed world the 'countryside', although visibly still green and apparently dominated by farming, is increasingly difficult to tell apart from 'urban' areas, at least as far as its people and their jobs are concerned.

Problems of rural areas in developing countries

Revised

- Rural areas used to be dominated by agriculture and other primary economic activities such as mining and forestry. In the developing world that is often still the case.

Knowing the basics

The profits made on large estates owned by foreign **transnational corporations** (TNCs) generally end up in developed countries.

Stretch and challenge

The problems facing many rural areas in the developing world can be summarised as follows:

- lack of opportunities – not enough jobs
- ill-health and poor education
- **isolation** and poor communications.

These tend to lead to economic decline as migration of the young and more motivated to cities reduces the productivity of rural areas.

Stretch and challenge

The developing world is not uniform. Some developing countries are now experiencing **suburbanisation** and commuting trends are very similar to those in the developed world.

Check your understanding

Tested

Give ONE reason why TNCs might be involved in agriculture in the developing countries.

Lake District

The Lake District is a **National Park** – in the UK these are not owned by the people and the only difference between them and other rural areas is that planning rules are even tighter.

- Home to about 45,000 people.
- A National Park with special **planning** laws.
- A very popular **tourism** and leisure destination – 15 million visitor-days per year.
- Nearly 20 per cent of houses are **second homes** – can be over 50 per cent in some villages.
- Nearly 30 per cent of the population is over 60 years of age – 10 per cent are over 75.

Malawi

- Population 13.9 million.
- Infant mortality 90 per 1000.
- 47 per cent of the population is under 15 years of age.
- Only 73 per cent of the population has access to safe drinking water.
- Adult literacy is 62 per cent.

examiner tip

There is a difference between what people want in their own lives and what might be good for the region. Remember 'Not in My Back Yard' – NIMBY. No one wants a prison built next door to them although some people might welcome it as it brings much-needed jobs to the area.

	A rural area in a developed country		A rural area in a developing country		
Issues	Why an issue?	On the ground in the Lake District	Issues	Why an issue?	On the ground in Malawi
Employment	Rural areas lack the range of job opportunities offered by cities. Traditionally these areas had primary jobs in agriculture, mining, forestry and fishing but many of these sectors are under pressure. Throughout Europe agriculture has been subsidised in the past but much less so today – imported raw materials are often cheaper than locally produced goods and so mining and forestry have also declined	The Lake District is dominated by one type of employment – nearly 40 per cent of the jobs are in hotels and restaurants – double the national figure, with another eight per cent working for the National Park. Otherwise there are a few more jobs in farming (nearly eight per cent) than the national average. Many tourism jobs are poorly paid and part-time. Many residents commute out of the park to work. There are a significant number of 'homeworkers' although broadband connectivity is patchy	Economic decline	Rural areas often have a limited range of activities and very few jobs outside farming and mining. The money made from these activities often goes to landowners. Prices for these products have been falling in recent years so farmers get lower incomes. In many poor countries the best land is owned by landlords who are wealthy enough from their rents not to worry too much about what is done with the land	Malawi is a very poor country. Most people live in rural areas. Only 11 per cent of GDP comes from industry and most of that is processing of agricultural products. Most of the land is owned by landlords who are often not interested in developing that land. Two million smallholder farmers cultivate on average a hectare compared with 30,000 estates cultivating 1.1 million hectares. Over 2.6 million hectares lies idle in the rural areas

	A rural area in a developed country			A rural area in a developing country		
Issues	Why an issue?	On the ground in the Lake District	Issues	Why an issue?	On the ground in Malawi
Housing	Providing affordable housing in rural areas is not easy. Local people often have lower wages than in urban areas and there are fewer 'brownfield' sites where development would be easy. Areas close to cities are affected by commuters who push up prices while tourist destinations are frequently affected by second-home ownership which tends to push up prices	The National Park is required to supply another 1000 homes by 2020. Without more housing it will be difficult to attract new businesses into the area. House prices are high in the region and second-home ownership is very high. These two are related – limited supply and high demand from outsiders. Many other properties are holiday cottages for rent	Isolation	Rural areas are often poorly served by road, rail and other forms of communication, most notably the internet. In poor countries phone links are rare and internet connectivity is unreliable. This lack of communication separates these areas from the world economy. As a result young people move away and few firms are interested in investing	In 2007 Malawi had one telephone for every 139 people and internet use was even worse – one for every 240 people. Most of this was in cities. Rural mobile coverage is also poor so the process that has taken place in some developing countries of mobiles being found almost everywhere is not yet true in Malawi. Isolation leads to rural decline. Malawi is landlocked and surrounded by other countries that face severe challenges
Tourism and leisure	Leisure and tourism can help the economy of rural areas by providing jobs and income. However, they also bring more negative impacts. The traffic congestion and the damage to the environment mean that the number of visitors is quite limited, especially in mountain areas where the landscape is more fragile. Tourists also change the types of services and shops provided, which is not always to the benefit of local people	Traffic congestion in the Lake District in summer is a problem. 90 per cent of visitors arrive by car. 72 per cent of visits are day trips and the vast majority arrive by car – only eight per cent are foreign visitors. Most visits are to towns and although 85 per cent of visitors walk, this is largely in towns. The shops and services in towns are geared to visitors who produce an income of over £600 million each year. Local people who have no income from tourism directly are sometimes negatively affected by traffic and changing services – gift shops replacing food shops	Rural population change	Rapid urbanisation has not really depopulated most rural areas in the developing world but the most able and skilled people often move away to cites or even abroad. This leaves rural areas with unbalanced populations with large numbers of dependants but fewer people of working age	Malawi is the least urbanised country in the world with 15.3 per cent of people living in urban areas. But its cities are growing much faster than its rural areas because of rural to urban migration. Rural populations are still growing but at a slow rate (0.5 per cent per year) compared with urban areas (six per cent per year)
The environment	There is a conflict here. If a rural region is to keep its young people from moving away, it needs to provide a range of jobs – this might mean small factories, it will certainly mean more housing and more services. Doing this without damaging tourism is not easy. It is also difficult to keep visitors from damaging the environment that they have come to see	54 per cent of the land area is farmed, with much of the rest rough moorland. Farms and tourists are not always a good mix, with damage done both by carelessness and occasional vandalism. Footpath erosion is a serious issue in popular places	A spoilt environment	Poor communities are often forced to destroy the environment just to survive. If the best land is reserved for a few then the rest will do what they can to survive. Each day rural farmers all over the world spend valuable time collecting firewood for cooking and the lack of good land means that over-farming and desertification are common in poorer areas	50,000–70,000 hectares of forest are being destroyed every year according to the Wildlife and Environmental Society of Malawi. In 2011 Mzuzu city was seriously damaged by hailstorms due to the lack of a tree cover acting as a windbreak in the city. Many people are still cutting trees for charcoal, fuel wood and timber despite the forest being legally protected

The pressures resulting from links between rural and urban areas in developed countries

- Urban rural links do not always bring benefits to rural areas, even in developed countries.
- Although life and death struggles are unknown, it is still fair to suggest that urban areas are the centres of power and national policies revolve around cities.
- In many developed countries rural areas are no longer dominated by farming as they once were. Some may suffer rural **depopulation** whereas other experience growth through **counter-urbanisation**.

The pressures on rural areas

Commuting and suburbanisation

- Commuters' wealth is not always spent in villages and rural areas.
- 3000 villages in the UK have no shop. Village post offices are closing at the rate of 400 a year. Pubs are disappearing, as are village schools. Incomers frequently shop in town and eat and drink at home.
- It is increasingly hard for local people to find affordable housing and planners are often unwilling to allow village growth into greenfield sites.

Knowing the basics

Commuting villages are usually within an hour of a major city.

Stretch and challenge

Rural areas may appear affluent but there are often pockets of considerable deprivation, especially for older and more vulnerable people.

Tourism and honeypots

- 'Going to the country' has been a popular pastime for well over 100 years, especially to visit pretty villages such as Corfe Castle in Dorset, and Lacock in Wiltshire.
- Many villages become living museums presenting a rural idyll. Village shops become gift shops, pubs become gastro-pubs and traffic congestion increases.
- Closer to cities, land-use changes are obvious with golf courses, country parks, paintballing and adventure activities.

Second homes and retirement migration

- In regions further from cities and generally seen as attractive, there has been a significant growth in second homes and people moving in after retirement.
- The south-west of England is an obvious example but so too is the Lake District.
- The impact is a little like that of suburbanisation but more severe. Houses are often left empty in winter and a mixture of retirement and second homes will have an impact on local services, not least the numbers of children in school.
- As houses are sought after, prices rise, while incomes remain low.

Knowing the basics

Very few rural areas in the developed world still rely on farming.

Stretch and challenge

National Parks are much misunderstood bodies – the areas are neither 'parks' nor 'national' given that they are largely privately owned.

Demand for resources

- Rural areas have always supplied resources to cities but these demands have increased.
- Past timber shortages have meant that pine forests have been planted in upland areas of the UK.
- In other areas, stone, sand and gravel are quarried.

The impact of the national and global economy on declining rural areas

Revised

- Rural areas are often neglected by governments. Sometimes deliberately, sometimes because they have so much more to do in large and rapidly growing urban areas.
- International treaties and agreements can limit what governments can do.
- In recent years globalisation has meant that even very remote rural areas have been affected by global policies.

examiner tip

Even poor countries have some rich people living in them and they often control these countries. They are often quite keen on policies that do not always favour the rest of the country.

Check your understanding

Tested

1 What is the suburbanisation of the countryside?

2 Complete the table below to show the impacts on your chosen rural region.

	Chosen declining rural area – developing country ....
Impact of national economy	Impact 1
	Impact 2
	Impact 3
Impact of **global economy**	Impact 1
	Impact 2
	Impact 3

How might these issues be resolved sustainably?

How to improve the economy of rural areas in developing countries

Revised

- The best way of helping the rural poor is to improve their health and education.
- Rural poverty cannot be solved by local initiatives alone because the global system may be the basic cause.
- The attempts to achieve a more sustainable future for these rural regions will be looked at in the next section.

Stretch and challenge

Rural areas are sometimes dominated by rich and powerful people who often live in the cities or even overseas.

Check your understanding

Tested

Fill in the case study box with details of four different rural initiatives for your chosen case study.

Rural region	
Initiative 1	
Initiative 1	
Initiative 3	
Initiative 4	

The future for rural Malawi – will it be sustainable? Revised

- We live in a globalised world. As a result it is not easy, maybe impossible, to achieve sustainability without some co-operation from national governments and international organisations.
- As it stands, Malawi's agricultural system is not sustainable, not least because of HIV/AIDS but also because:
  - 'Meeting the needs of the present …' – Malawi has high levels of malnutrition and poor diet
  - '… Without compromising the ability of future generations to meet their own needs' – export crops such as tobacco and tea are flown thousands of miles to market. Too many smallholders crowded into the remaining countryside are forced to grow crops where the land is not suitable and poverty forces deforestation.

Feeding Malawi's population is a goal of the government and it has two major projects that might help it achieve that. This does not necessarily help the country become more sustainable except in a political and social sense.

Project 1 – Using the lake

- Drought is a persistent problem for Malawi. Rainfall varies considerably both seasonally and from year to year. The country has one of the most unpredictable rainfall patterns in Africa.
- Between 1967 and 2003, the country experienced six major droughts, affecting over 21 million people. Floods occur in southern Malawi, particularly in the Lower Shire River valley and the lakeshore areas of Lake Malawi.
- One way to improve the reliability of the water supply would be to use the lake. Lake Malawi is the size of Wales and using its waters for irrigation would increase yields in a wide strip of land along the lakeshore.
- Opponents are critical of the possible impact on fish stocks and the environment.

Project 2 – GM crops

- The Malawi government has been an enthusiastic supporter of genetically modified (GM) crops. In general the development of GM crops has concentrated on crops grown in the developed world. Malawi's main crop just happens to be maize (or corn as it is called in the USA) which has probably had more GM research than any other.
- Just like the green revolution that changed farming 40 years ago in many developing countries, companies such as Monsanto hope that GM will do the same. They do this to make a profit and it is not clear whether GM crops will be good for Malawi – they increase dependency on foreign firms because both seeds and fertiliser are imported. Although they increase yield, so too do much simpler and much cheaper changes in farm techniques.

Is sustainability achievable?

- It all depends on what we mean by sustainability. If Malawi's rural population becomes healthier and wealthier, they may also start consuming more.
- At the moment, poor rural regions of Africa have the lowest eco-footprints on Earth. If they rise in the future then the people may be better fed and happier but they will almost certainly have a greater impact on the planet.

'Haiti, Afghanistan and Malawi are the countries with the smallest ecological footprints, under 0.5 global hectares and, in most cases, too small to meet basic requirements for food, shelter, infrastructure and sanitation.'

Source: http://www.footprintnetwork.org/en/index.php/newsletter/bv/new_data_shows_humanitys_ecological_debt_compounding

Knowing the basics

Sustainable development should look after the present generation as a priority.

Stretch and challenge

Any agricultural system that has large estates devoted to export crops that use up the best land is unlikely to be helping the ordinary farmers.

Check your understanding

Tested ☐

What are GM crops?

How to improve the economy of rural areas in developed countries

Revised ☐

- The problem for rural areas in developed countries is not keeping people alive but keeping people there. Many rural areas have experienced rural depopulation in the past and even today growth is most obviously through counter-urbanisation in rural areas close to cities. In these places the jobs are urban, the society is urban and the countryside just provides a backdrop for urban lifestyles.

- Most countries value their rural living spaces and want to preserve them because they are culturally important. The idea of a countryside empty of people is not one that most governments are comfortable with.

- So the trick is to keep people in rural areas and to do what is needed to encourage diversification.

Rural initiatives in the Lake District

1 Developing tourism. Tourism is already the largest industry in the Lake District but it has become more diverse in recent years. Many tourist enterprises are owned by people who live outside the region so the profits too go outside the region – a process known as leakage.

There are several opportunities to increase tourist income and keep it in the region – one plan would allow development of adventure parks and outdoor pursuits just outside the park boundaries. Another is to help keep money in the area. A good example of a more sustainable form of tourism is Honister Mine: 'Honister is owned by a local family and is a supporter of the Lake District community, economy and the environment. Every penny you spend at Honister helps support the mine and our young people' (*source*: www.honister.com).

2 Farm diversification. Hill farming has never been an easy life, but since the EU has lowered grants it has become much more marginal. Modern farming methods have reduced the need to use difficult environments such as mountains, with a lot of meat now being produced by lowland farmers. A good example of diversification is Low Sizergh Farm: 'The eighteenth-century stone barn on this dairy farm is full of speciality foods from Cumbria and beyond including cheeses, meats, superb homemade cakes and organic eggs and vegetables from the farm. The tea room makes good use of the wonderful local produce from the farm shop. You can watch the cows being milked daily around 1.15p.m. from the tea room's viewing window. Browse in the craft galleries and stroll on the farm trail' (*source*: www.lowsizerghbarn.co.uk).

3 Development of the knowledge economy. The development of a high-quality business location geared towards the knowledge economy offers the chance to provide well-paid employment within the area. Nationally, forecasts are for strong employment growth in the knowledge-based sectors. However, the Lake District currently has a very low share of these sectors. Tourism and agriculture are relatively lowly paid so there is a need to develop high-value employment in and around the National Park. The loss of well-paid jobs at Sellafield, GlaxoSmithKline and BAE Systems will further damage the Lake District's economic base. The Kendal area offers the best opportunity for the development of the knowledge-based industries due to its excellent strategic transport connections. This location would also help business collaboration with the research facilities of Lancaster University. These are just plans and not likely to be a reality for some time.

Figure 1 Many rural areas have campaigned to get reliable and fast internet access. The remote locations of some communities mean that the costs are high.

Knowing the basics

Some tourism is better for the environment than others – walking holidays and eco-tourism do less damage than touring by car.

Stretch and challenge

People who move into rural regions to retire often have different ideas about the best future for these regions than young residents seeking jobs and houses.

Check your understanding

What is the knowledge economy?

Tested ☐

The future for rural areas – will they be sustainable?

- Rural areas in developed countries face challenges but the nature of those challenges is very uncertain.
- For the past 40 years globalisation has had an impact in that large farms have become larger with the growth of agribusiness while smaller family-owned farms have found it harder to compete. Many smaller farms have gone, either absorbed by the bigger farms or bought up by urban migrants who have then rented out the land.
- Villages have lost services. They have become less like communities and more like places where people just live quite close together in a rural area.
- As it stands, rural areas will not be sustainable unless things change:
  - 'Meeting the needs of the present ...' – to do this there needs to be a wider range of job opportunities and housing. Both are critical but may be in conflict with other goals such as the preservation of the landscape and the needs of tourists and visitors. There are almost always winners and losers from development and that is certainly the case here.
  - '... Without compromising the ability of future generations to meet their own needs' – the future generations are leaving Britain's remote rural areas and they will not return unless job opportunities develop. Rural areas have always supplied labour to cities and that is unlikely to change.

Check your understanding

Tested

1 Fill in the table below with details of two sustainable projects from your chosen rural region.

Rural region	
Sustainable project 1	
Sustainable project 2	

Is sustainability achievable?

Once again it all depends on what we mean by sustainability.

- Areas such as the Lake District could not become a self-contained community that requires no support from outside, however successful its energy programme might be in the future. Too many people depend for their living on visitors. But it could edge closer by reducing its carbon footprint – stressing different forms of transport and changing some of the land management.
- Wealthy retired people are likely to go on retiring here and second homes are unlikely to disappear. Whether second-home ownership is just not sustainable if you want to look after 'the needs of the present' is a good question. The definition below is different to the one on page 20.

'Sustainable development is based on the idea that the quality of people's lives and the state of our communities, are affected by economic, social and environmental factors. The links between them influence our quality of life now and in the future.'
Source: Lake District National Park Authority.

Knowing the basics

Developing sustainable energy is especially promising in areas with high winds and rainfall such as the Lake District.

Stretch and challenge

It will be a considerable challenge to keep young people in rural regions when jobs are neither varied nor often well paid.

Check your understanding

Tested

2 What is sustainable energy?

Exam focus

1 Identify TWO causes of rural decline. [2]

2 Outline ONE reason why rural areas might lose population. [2]

3 Describe ONE way in which national governments can affect rural areas. [2]

4 Using a named country, explain how the global economy affects its rural economy. [4]

5 With reference to a developed country, explain the problems of housing in rural areas. [4]

6 Identify TWO reasons why employment opportunities are limited in rural areas. [2]

7 Describe the costs and benefits of tourism for rural areas in the developed world. [4]

8 Outline ONE disadvantage of growing commuting populations in rural communities. [2]

9 Identify ONE obstacle to rural development in many rural areas in developing countries. [2]

10 With reference to a named country, describe TWO attempts to improve rural economies. [4]

11 Define the term 'sustainable rural development'. [2]

12 For a named country, describe how rural sustainability might be achieved in the developing world. [4]

13 Outline ONE attempt to diversify rural economies. [2]

14 Give ONE reason why internet connectivity is so important for rural areas. [2]

15 State TWO reasons why sustainable rural development is hard to achieve in the developed world. [2]

16 Describe ONE attempt to make rural areas in the developed world more sustainable. [4]

Answers online

Section C Large-scale People and the Planet
Chapter 7 Development Dilemmas
How and why do countries develop in different ways?

Regional disparity

- There are many reasons why some regions of a country are richer than other regions just as there are many reasons why, on average, some countries are richer than others.

- London and its surrounding area has been the richest region of the UK for well over 1000 years. The original reasons for this are no longer relevant but other factors have kept up these initial advantages and made sure that they continue.

- Initial advantages may include: soil fertility and climate, availability of water, ability to trade, port facilities, centre for government.

Knowing the basics

Richer regions have often been richer for a long time, many centuries in some cases. Regional differences persist.

Check your understanding

Tested

Outline ONE reason why a region might be rich.

Figure 1 The location of Maharashtra and Bihar in India

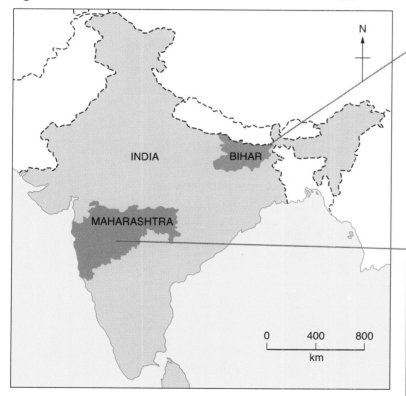

Bihar is very rural – 80 per cent of the population lives in rural areas. Income is only 20 per cent of that in Maharashtra. The reasons include:
- Despite fertile soils, many farmers have no land of their own and produce little more than they need for themselves.
- There is a very wide gap between rich and poor. Patna – the biggest city – is one of India's richest cities.
- Government is more corrupt than elsewhere in India.
- There are very few industries, education is poor and the birth rate high.

Maharashtra is one of the richest regions in India, mostly because of Mumbai, which is one of India's largest and most successful cities. It is a centre for:
- Services such as banking and insurance including many telephone call centres.
- Manufacturing industry from steel to textiles.
- 'Bollywood' – the Indian centre for film-making – is the best-known example of its entertainment and leisure industry.
- Administration and government – cities such as Mumbai are centres for government, often with well-paid jobs.

Stretch and challenge

There is often as much variation within regions as there is between them. Maharashtra has many very poor rural areas that are less fertile and more affected by out-migration of farmers than in Bihar.

The impact of differences between rich cities and the poor countryside

Revised

- The most important movement of people on the planet is still people moving from rural to urban regions.
- In India and China, this movement is driven by poverty and rural deprivation.
- Urban **core** economies are growing faster than rural **peripheral** ones and are predicted to carry on doing so. There are more jobs; there is a wider variety of jobs including some that are better paid. There are more opportunities in the informal economy. There are more educational opportunities and often better health care. Even the living conditions might be better, bad though they are in the slums and shanty towns.
- In Bihar, as in many other Indian states, rich landlords live in the cities. Poor farmers do not own their land and cannot invest in it. Having many children is seen as a route out of poverty and migration is another.
- By some estimates, 400 million Indians will migrate from rural to urban areas in the next 40 years. In Europe a similar-sized migration took 1000 years.

Figure 2 Vicious cycle of poverty

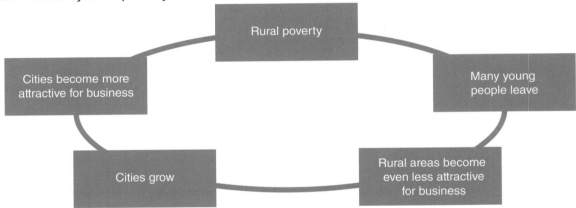

- As the cycle in Figure 2 shows, urban cores keep growing and the rural periphery struggles. As a result the development gap grows between these regions and within the regions too, with urban areas such as Mumbai performing much better than the rest of Maharashtra.
- The **human development index (HDI)** data below shows the gap between Mumbai in India's richest state and Bihar, the poorest state in India.

	Mumbai	Bihar
Income per capita per year (converted to £)	£11,000	£77
Literacy (%)	85.6	64.0
Life expectancy (years)	71	65

- The central business district (CBD) of Mumbai has offices and businesses that offer a wide range of jobs and opportunities. These might not be well paid by developed world standards, but they are high for India. Mumbai has plans to become a city to stand alongside Singapore, Hong Kong and Shanghai as an international business centre.
- Rural Bihar is one of the poorest regions in India, relying on rice and vegetable crops from small plots of rented land. There are few other resources in this fertile region; most villages have no electricity, use dung for fuel and only a few children are educated.

examiner tip

Remember that the main aim of development is to make people healthier and happier – not necessarily richer.

Tested

Check your understanding

What is the human development index?

The differences between top-down development and bottom-up development

Revised

- There are many ways to encourage economic development in poor regions. They vary from enormous projects that are truly national in scale to micro projects that may just help a few families.
- Project types have been grouped into two main categories: top-down projects and bottom-up projects.

	Top-down development	Bottom-up development
Scale	Frequently large, involving a region or large area	Often small – village or small area
Control	Usually planned and organised by the central government in the capital city	Usually organised and controlled by the local community
Technology	Often highly technical with much imported machinery and technical support	Often use intermediate technology that is simpler and needs less technical support
Cost and finance	These often cost huge amounts and are sometimes financed by foreign loans and foreign institutions such as the World Bank	These are sometimes very cheap indeed. Finance can be local even in poor regions
Environmental impact	Because these projects are large the impact will almost always be widespread. They don't necessarily have negative impacts but some do. Of course, the planners of these projects rarely have to live with the consequences	Because these projects are small the impacts are less, although a large number of small projects may have an impact that is not so different from one large one. The difference is that the planners have to live with the consequences
Example	The Three Gorges Dam on the Yangtze River in China is one of the best-known top-down projects of recent years – it cost about $30 billion	Biogas projects produce methane gas from cow dung. The kit can be bought and installed for as little as $200 per household

Tested

Check your understanding

Define the term 'bottom-up development'.

The impact of the Three Gorges project on different groups of people

Figure 3 China's electricity production by source

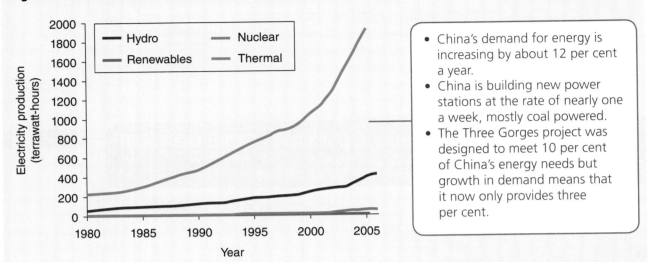

- China's demand for energy is increasing by about 12 per cent a year.
- China is building new power stations at the rate of nearly one a week, mostly coal powered.
- The Three Gorges project was designed to meet 10 per cent of China's energy needs but growth in demand means that it now only provides three per cent.

The Three Gorges Dam is the largest in the world. The lake, when filled, will have a surface area of 1000 km². The aim was to:

- produce electricity by using hydropower
- offer flood control on the lower Yangtze below the dam, a notorious area for flooding
- improve trade by allowing navigation on the upper Yangtze.

The Three Gorges generates electricity for the Chinese electricity grid, powering factories and homes around the country.

Critics point out that:

- The dam will lead to loss of species below the dam such as river dolphins.
- The lake will become toxic with waste seeping in from the ground.
- Eutrophication will take place as the water stops flowing through the lake and backs up in tributaries.
- Farming below the dam needs the flood waters for growing rice.
- The lake will silt up in 50 years and flood control will get more difficult.
- 1.4 million people have lost their homes.
- The dam is built on fault lines in an earthquake zone – catastrophic failure would put at risk some of the 75 million people who live downstream.

It is obvious that every project has its winners and losers. Some people benefit; some do not. This is true of the Three Gorges project.

Winners	Losers
The people who get jobs at the dam and with the power companies	The 1.4 million people who had to move from their homes
The people who run the companies managing the project who made money from its construction	The fishing communities who find their fish stocks either gone or reduced both behind the dam and downstream
The people of China breathing in just a little less polluted air from the coal-fired power stations that would have been needed if the dam had not been built	The communities downstream protected from flooding have less available water for irrigation of rice fields which has been fed by river flooding for centuries

How might countries develop more sustainably in the future?

The characteristics of bottom-up development projects

Revised ▢

	Details and examples
Scale	Some schemes are local in scale but have a central organisation. One such scheme is the Grameen Bank, which supplies very small loans specifically for bottom-up development projects. This micro-credit system started in Bangladesh but now operates in many other countries, making it international yet locally focused
Control	Local communities are not always democratic. Village leaders are seldom elected in African states and not all bottom-up schemes consult all villagers. A recent survey in Vietnam showed that only 13 per cent of peasant farmers thought that greater local involvement was an aim of bottom-up projects
Technology	Intermediate technology is cheaper, simpler and easier to service. In recent years a lot of attention has been paid to developing technology that does not use fossil fuels but employs solar energy instead
Cost and finance	Many bottom-up schemes cost very little and micro-credit schemes can allow local businesses to start up or expand. Finance can come from micro-finance organisations, such as the Grameen Bank, that make loans to groups of individuals making each of them responsible for the debt. Many borrowers are women
Environmental impact	Obviously, each bottom-up project has much less impact than top-down projects, just because they are so much smaller. It is much more difficult to judge whether the impact is less if you add up the impacts of many small projects. In principle, because bottom-up projects use local materials they have a lower environmental impact

Check your understanding

Tested ▢

1 What is intermediate technology?

Bottom-up development in rural India

- One of the best-known bottom-up projects in rural India is the introduction of the biogas systems that have changed rural life.
- Each biogas digester costs between $500 and $1000 for each household. Cow dung – cows produce about 10 tonnes a year – and also human waste are used. Both cooking gas and gas for lighting are provided by the digester.

Figure 4 A schematic drawing of a biogas plant

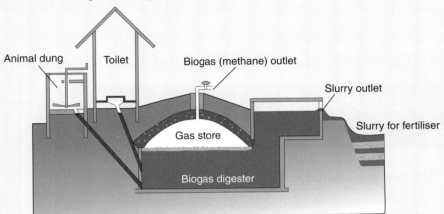

The problem:

- In Indian villages the main fuel has been firewood. However, this is in increasingly short supply with more than 30 kg needed each week for each family.
- Cow dung is also used as a fuel, especially as firewood is taking longer to collect.
- Cow dung is a better fertiliser than a fuel and burning cow dung produces health problems.
- Women are largely responsible for collecting fuel and cooking. With more and more time taken up, few girls can spend time at school.
- Lack of lighting in homes limits opportunities for reading in the evening.

The solution:

- Bio-digesters have been used for many years – there are over six million in rural China and four million in India.
- They produce methane gas and slurry for fertiliser.
- The time saved in not collecting firewood allows girls to go to school – an important stage in economic development.
- The bio-digesters are relatively easy to construct and cheap to maintain.
- The bio-digesters reduce disease because less smoke is inhaled and fermenting the dung in the biogas digester kills the disease-causing microorganisms.
- They create jobs – building and maintaining biogas plants employs about 250,000 people in India.
- They can be used to generate electricity to pump water.

The limitations:

- In India the cities are growing very rapidly – biogas plants cannot help the energy crisis in cities as the system needs animals to work.
- The initial costs may be low but they still need to be met – in some rural areas money is very difficult to find.

Knowing the basics

Bottom-up schemes help women out by saving them time.

Check your understanding

2 Identify TWO benefits of biogas for local communities.

Tested

How sustainable is rural development?

Sustainable development is a fairly new idea – it was first defined back in 1987 when a United Nations (UN) committee looking at the problems of development offered this definition:

Development that meets the need of the present without compromising the ability of future generations to meet their own needs.

The UN went on to stress that the priority was to make sure that present poverty was addressed. Since the idea of sustainability was first launched, it has been used very widely without always having much meaning: sustainable schools, sustainable companies, sustainable profit and so on.

Measuring sustainable development is not easy but the following seven golden rules could be helpful.

1 Allow local people to have a say.
2 Be affordable and not involve large loans and debt.
3 Be good for human health.
4 Allow the environment to flourish.
5 Minimise waste and pollution.
6 Reduce, or at least limit, demand for resources such as fuel and water.
7 Make sure poor people benefit as much as or more than rich people.

The problem:

● Rural India, like rural China, is poorer than the urban areas and so has a smaller impact on the environment – a lower eco-footprint.

● As a result rural areas are more sustainable. However, as rural areas develop it is likely that they will use more resources and become less sustainable.

● Economic development involves people becoming richer and as they do so they consume more products.

● Rural India is changing fast. However, more commercial farming methods with larger farms and fewer workers and more machines are not more sustainable.

● As an example, Tata Motors developed the Tata Nano – India's so-called people's car. It costs a little more than £1400 and is aimed at the growing number of Indians in both town and country who wish to exchange two wheels (mostly bicycles) for four. The prospect of Indians owing cars in far greater numbers is understandable but bad for sustainability.

Knowing the basics

Rural development is difficult because there is a lack of variety in employment.

Stretch and challenge

Sustainable development should look after the needs of the present and address poverty – much of that poverty is in the rural world.

Check your understanding

Tested

Define the term 'sustainable development'.

Top-down or bottom-up schemes – which are better?

The answer is that every country needs both. But the following points are clear:

- Bottom-up development can be important in helping local communities.
- Bottom-up development can bring important benefits to some especially vulnerable groups such as children and women.
- But bottom-up development played a very limited role in the development of the rich countries of the world. On the contrary, they developed with large-scale government-led projects and policies.
- The main reason why countries such as China and South Korea have developed so rapidly is the important part played by small- and medium-sized enterprises (SMEs).
- Bigger enterprises enjoy real savings through what is called economies of scale, producing cheaper goods more efficiently than lots of small businesses.
- Countries need an infrastructure – that is a skeleton of communication, power supply and flows of information. These cannot be provided by bottom-up projects.

Knowing the basics

Top-down schemes are often very expensive.

Stretch and challenge

You need top-down schemes to bind a country together – to provide the communications and the networks that allow bottom-up schemes to flourish.

Kerala, India

Kerala in southern India is India's richest rural region. 32 million people live there with an average income of under $300 per person per year. Yet the development indicators compare well with developed economies.

Development indicator	Kerala	India as a whole	The lowest income countries	USA
Adult literacy (%)	91	61	39	96
Life expectancy (male, years)	69	67	59	74
Life expectancy (female, years)	76	72	63	80
Infant mortality per 1000	10	33	80	7
Birth rate per 1000	17	21	40	16

So Kerala has statistics that make it hard to decide whether it is more like the rest of India than the USA. How has it achieved this? Is it bottom-up development?

The reasons are listed below:

Policy	Top-down or bottom-up
Land reform giving ownership to small farmers	Top-down – a government policy
Investment in education	Top-down with local community co-operation
Women's rights	Top-down with local community co-operation
Development of public services	Top-down – a government policy
Abolition of caste system	Top-down – resisted by some local communities

Kerala is a success story largely because of government-led policies that have had a good deal of local community support. So top-down with a bottom-up response.

1. Study Figure 1 on page 61. Describe the pattern of income in India. [3]

2. Outline ONE reason why rural areas are often poor. [2]

3. Study Figure 2 on page 62. Explain why very poor rural regions seem to be trapped in a vicious circle. [3]

4. Outline ONE reason why life expectancy is often lower in rural regions in the developing world. [2]

5. Identify TWO features of top-down development projects. [2]

6. For a project that you have studied, outline ONE possible weakness of bottom-up development projects. [2]

7. Study Figure 3 on page 64. Describe the changes in China's electricity production. [3]

8. For a top-down development project that you have studied explain why there are always winners and losers. [6]

9. Define the term 'intermediate technology'. [2]

10. Outline TWO characteristics of bottom-up development projects. [4]

11. For a bottom-up development project that you have studied, state TWO economic benefits of this scheme. [4]

12. Give ONE reason why bottom-up projects might be more suitable for poor rural areas. [2]

13. Identify TWO features of sustainable rural development projects. [2]

14. Outline ONE reason why eco-footprints in developing countries are likely to rise in the future. [2]

15. For a country or region that you have studied, compare the contribution of top-down and bottom-up developments to its development. [6]

Answers online

Chapter 8 World of Work

How does the 'new economy' function in different places? Who wins and who loses?

The changing geography of the global economy
Revised ☐

- The Clark–Fisher model (see page 31) shows that economies change over time with the balance between different types of employment changing.

- The background to these changes in the past 30 years has been the process known as **globalisation**. Globalisation is often defined as 'the greater integration of the global economy'.

- This means that:
  - fewer and fewer countries try to develop economies that are self-sufficient
  - countries prefer to specialise in those economic activities to which they are best suited
  - each country takes on different roles in the global economy
  - rich, developed countries concentrate on what has sometimes been called the **knowledge economy**, producing the research, ideas and financial services
  - financial services are concentrated in and around global cities such as London, New York and Tokyo
  - manufacturing and lower paid service jobs are concentrated in the newly industrial countries, most commonly China but also India and other newly industrialised countries
  - some countries in the developing world concentrate on the production of raw materials.

- This organisation of world production is known as the **new economy**, especially that part of it that refers to changes in the economy of developed countries such as the UK and the USA.

Figure 1 The flow of goods and services through an economy

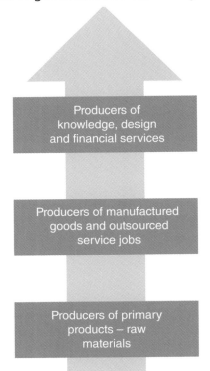

Producers of knowledge, design and financial services

Producers of manufactured goods and outsourced service jobs

Producers of primary products – raw materials

> **examiner tip**
>
> All topics have definitions to remember – in this one, the most obvious is the meaning of the term 'new economy'.

- These changes are a result of the processes involved in globalisation. There are several key players in this process.

Players	Policies
Global organisations such as the International Monetary Fund and World Bank	Lend money to governments to develop in a certain way and encourage free trade
Transnational corporations (TNCs)	Look to make profit by reducing production costs
Governments of rich, developed countries	Reduce taxes on companies and rich people, privatise businesses
Some governments in poorer developing countries	Encourage TNCs to invest in their countries – develop the primary sector such as mining and agriculture

Globalisation is very controversial:

- Those in favour say that it has increased global wealth for all.
- Those opposed say it has made rich people richer at the expense of poor people.

Knowing the basics

The global economy is important because most countries now trade with other countries.

Stretch and challenge

International institutions have encouraged more global connections between countries because this policy has been profitable to TNCs and richer countries.

Check your understanding

Tested

What is the 'global economy'?

The impact of the new economy on different groups of people

Revised

- Globally, the picture is fairly clear. Rich countries have certainly got richer, on average, while poor countries have not made much progress at all (see Figure 2 on page 72).
- But obviously the populations in a country (any country) do not all earn the average income. There are winners and losers within countries. The gap between rich and poor has increased within countries as well as between them.
- In developing countries there have been winners too:
  - The rich minority, especially landowners, with natural resources such as oil and minerals.
  - Those who get jobs in the industries that moved their operations to developing countries (**outsourcing**).
- There are other costs too, not least the environmental damage done to developing countries with primary and secondary industries creating high levels of pollution.
- Of the world's top 20 polluted cities, 15 are in China and India, both rapidly developing economies. Linfen, in China, has birth defects 30 times the global average. These people are also losers from the **global shift**.

Figure 2 Global income changes 1980–2000

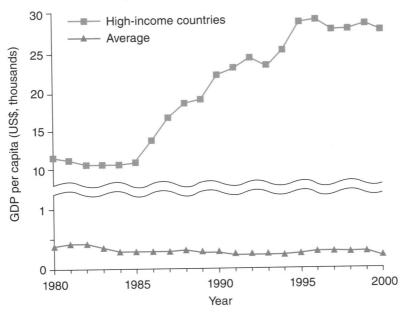

Why the rich have got richer?

- Tax cuts.
- Higher salaries for top-earners.
- More money from stocks and shares as TNCs make big profits.

Knowing the basics

In general terms, the past 30 years have seen the rich get richer and the poor have made little progress.

Stretch and challenge

The new economy has benefited a minority of people in developed countries. Don't forget that there are many poor people in developed countries. Nearly one in 10 Americans live in trailers (what we call caravans).

Check your understanding

Tested ☐

What does the term 'new economy' mean?

Transnational corporations – what they are and what they do

Revised ☐

Transnational corporations (TNCs) are:

- Companies that operate in more than one country.
- Often owned by shareholders.
- Run by company managers who have to look after the interest of the owners (shareholders) by making as much money as they can.
- Found in all sectors of the economy from primary to quaternary.

Sector	Example of a company	What they do	Where they do it
Primary	BHP Billiton	Mining and oil	Headquarters: UK and Australia Production: all over the world, where the raw materials are found Sales: all over the world to industries
Secondary	Levi-Strauss	Textiles and clothing	Headquarters: USA Production: Latin America (especially Mexico), China and south Asia
Tertiary	News Corporation	Media: newspapers, films and TV	Headquarters: USA Production: most continents for newspapers and TV; films distributed to all continents
Quaternary	Amgen	Biotechnology: drug research and production	Headquarters: USA Production: Puerto Rico, Netherlands, Ireland and the USA

Levi-Strauss

- A US company that makes clothing. Its best-known products are 501 jeans and Drifter pants.
- Up until 1998 it produced all of its clothing in the USA but was losing market share to its competitors. In 1998 it closed all but one of its US factories and moved production to Mexico. Thousands of jobs were lost in the USA; for example the small town of Blue Ridge (2000 inhabitants) lost 400 jobs, mostly jobs held by women.
- That followed a trend; in 1950 1.2 million Americans worked in clothing, again mostly women. By 2010 that figure had fallen to less than 200,000.
- Clothing and footwear are particularly likely to move overseas as labour is an important part of the costs – as much as 15–20 per cent of the cost of the product.

TNCs are very large organisations:

- The top 200 companies have sales that are larger than the GDP of many countries.
- Their total sales are responsible for more than 25 per cent of global economic activity.
- Much global trade is intra-corporate – between parts of one company or between companies.

To make more money, TNCs seek to reduce the cost of production and to gain a dominant market position, which helps them to control markets. This aids profit, which is good for shareholders but may not be quite so good for other people.

Knowing the basics

Primary industries in developing countries are often controlled by TNCs and the profit returns to the 'home' country.

Stretch and challenge

TNCs are owned by shareholders – these individuals and institutions do not have any loyalty to countries and will move their investment if it is profitable to do so.

Check your understanding

Tested ☐

Define the term 'transnational corporations'.

The advantages and disadvantages of TNCs for different groups in different places

Revised ☐

TNCs operate in all the main sectors of the economy: primary, secondary, tertiary and quaternary. They have important connections to government and spend large amounts of money on lobbying, public relations and advertising:

● Lobbying is an attempt to persuade governments to act in such a way as to increase corporation profits.

● Public relations is an attempt to build goodwill between a company and the public at large by improving its image.

● Advertising is usually intended to increase market share for a product by selling more of it.

TNCs are not 'people' – they are large companies. They bring advantages and disadvantages to groups of people and individuals so there are winners and losers in the same country. Four hundred women may have lost their jobs in Blue Ridge but shareholders in Levi-Strauss living in nearby Atlanta would benefit from the increased profits, the increased value of their shares and better dividends.

	Advantages	**Disadvantages**
Developed countries	• Cheap products for consumers • Some research and development jobs • Better environment as dirty industries move overseas • High salaries for executives and senior managers • Many jobs in lower paid areas of finance and business services • Profits for shareholders	• High job losses especially in manufacturing and tertiary services (**call centres**) • Decline of communities that once relied on these jobs, so a negative multiplier effect
Developing countries	• Jobs created where none existed before – relatively highly paid • Multiplier effect of this may lead to economic growth • Increasing skills in population may attract more new jobs • Significant gains for political leaders who sign deals with TNCs • Significant gains for landowners with resources	• Labour conditions are often poor and workers may be exploited • Poor health and safety standards • Jobs can disappear as cheap-labour areas compete • Pollution and waste spoil the environment • Rural–urban migration creates housing problems in cities and pressures in rural areas

The disadvantages of TNC operations are perhaps sometimes easier to see than the advantages, especially in developing countries. It is important to remember that there is a geography of profit. Many individuals benefit from the operation of TNCs, although it is not always as clear whether the poor and disadvantaged benefit greatly.

Knowing the basics

The main winners of TNC operations are to be found in the developed countries, although not in communities that used to make things.

examiner tip

Try to give examples – we all know lots of TNCs. If you are struggling, just think about your trainers or your last fast-food meal!

Stretch and challenge

Some individuals in developing countries benefit from the operations of TNCs – these individuals are usually the people in power.

Check your understanding

Tested ☐

Identify TWO groups of people who benefit from the operation of TNCs.

How sustainable might the future world of work be?

The impact of a growing service economy on developing countries

Revised

- Manufacturing jobs have been moving to developing countries for many years. It started as a slow process but it is now very common; service jobs have followed. This process is known as outsourcing.

- There are many reasons why companies outsource but also some potential risks. The main motive for service industries is, as with manufacturing industries, the attempt to reduce costs (see Figure 3).

Figure 3 The pros and cons of outsourcing

Pros
- Lower costs – cheap labour
- Focus on your main business
- Build foundations in another country
- Get a better service

Cons
- Loss of contact with customers
- Sensitive information might be vulnerable

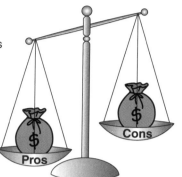

Outsourcing in India

- Over one million jobs.
- $61 billion in revenue.
- Five per cent of total GDP.
- Bangalore the centre of the industry.

Why India?

- Large pool of low-cost computer-literate English-speaking professionals (two million college graduates per year).
- Strong technical and maths skills. India has over 270 universities and 2400 colleges specialising in science, technology, finance, business and engineering.
- Labour costs are between one-tenth and one-fifth of the wages earned by information technology workers in the USA (see the table).
- India has the world's fifth largest public sector telecommunications network.
- Reliable satellite and submarine communications links.
- India has a well-developed banking system.
- Democratic government and political stability.
- Severe punishments for cybercrimes.

Job	US wage rate	Indian wage rate
Telephone operator	$12.57	$1.00
Legal assistant	$17.86	$7.00
Accountant	$23.35	$8.00
Software designer	$60.00	$6.00

The future?

- Indian companies appear to be offering more and more sophisticated services such as computer chip design, information technology services, design and architecture.
- US transnationals such as IBM and General Electric have established research and development centres in India.
- The USA's General Electric corporation's second largest research centre is located in Bangalore, with a staff of over 2000.
- Indian companies such as Infosys are now outsourcing to Europe. Tata, India's largest TNC, has call centres in Britain.

Knowing the basics

The main advantage of developing countries for companies that wish to outsource is the low cost of labour.

Stretch and challenge

The importance of English-speaking countries is significant for outsourcing and that helps India take a leading role in the growing service economy.

Check your understanding

Tested

Define the term 'outsourcing'.

The costs and benefits of outsourcing

Revised

- This is very much the same story as the advantages and disadvantages of TNC operations (see page 74), but with the difference that outsourced service jobs are sometimes more highly skilled and provide a few more opportunities.
- There is a geographical difference in that outsourcing of service jobs is more restricted than manufacturing.
- If you look at the Indian case study, issues such as the banking system and the communication network are more important to these service jobs than they are to manufacturing. Bangladesh is an attractive destination for TNCs looking for cheap labour, for example in the clothing industry, but it does not have the skills or infrastructure of neighbouring India so it attracts few outsourced service jobs.

Stretch and challenge

The main motive for outsourcing has been to save money for companies. If Indian wages increase in the future then it is possible that they will no longer be competitive. This may already be happening with the growth of Indian corporations.

Benefits – the winners	Problems – the losers
Services should be cheaper to customers in developed countries	Loss of jobs in developed countries so growth in numbers unemployed
Jobs provided to workers in the developing countries such as India	Antisocial working conditions and working times may create resentment to workers in developing countries
The multiplier effect of these new jobs creates more employment	Skilled workers in developed countries are also losing jobs
Greater understanding of Western values and attitudes by exposure to this culture	Loss of cultural identity for many people – workers and consumers in developing countries
Shareholders of outsourcing companies make more money	
High-wage employees and managers of the same companies as they get bigger bonuses	
Managers of outsourcing companies in the developing world	

Knowing the basics

There are winners from outsourcing in both developed and developing countries although the balance is uneven.

Check your understanding

Tested

State ONE advantage and ONE disadvantage of outsourcing.

The changing workplace

The death of the office? This obituary for the office was written in 2010.

'The office workplace that has dominated business since the nineteenth century is dying and most employees would be quite happy not to work in it, a global study by networking giant Cisco has found.

'This is a striking theme of the Cisco Connected World Report, which found that 60 per cent of employees from 2600 surveyed across 13 countries do not think it necessary to be in an office to be productive.

'An even greater number, 66 per cent, would be prepared to work for lower pay if a job offered more flexibility, at least when compared with a better-paid job without such flexibility.'

Source: http://news.techworld.com/mobile-wireless/3244829/ global-survey-predicts-death-of-the-office/

- Tertiary jobs dominate the developed economies and a shift to homeworking would be significant and important not least for the UK, with finance and business services providing something close to 60 per cent of jobs in London and the south-east of England.
- Many tertiary jobs are not mobile, for example jobs in retailing.
- But even in the tertiary sector change is taking place through, for example, the growth of the internet and broadband connectivity.

Knowing the basics
Fewer people may work in offices in the future as teleworking grows.

Stretch and challenge
Loss of 'back office' jobs to countries such as India makes the future of the service economy very uncertain.

Check your understanding

1 Complete the table by providing your own example or extra detail.

Change	Impact	Comment/Example
Robotisation	The replacement of people with machines has now become the replacement of people with computers and robots	....
Internet and broadband connectivity	There are connected and unconnected places. The knowledge-based economy of quaternary services relies on connectivity with a possible growth of homeworking as the office declines	....
Internet retailing	The growth of internet retailing may have an impact on jobs in the traditional retail sector	....
Temporary and part-time working	As the location of work has become more flexible, secure, long-term jobs have decreased in number	....
The topsy-turvy world of information technology skills	Indian information technology firms are now starting to outsource to the USA	....

2 State ONE reason why information technology jobs are growing in countries such as India.

Will it all last?

- The changing geography of the world-wide economy was an obvious impact of globalisation. Globalisation was a set of processes largely controlled by the developed world.

- The developed world retained control of the local economy of developing countries because it controlled the research and design of new products and the flow of capital (money). Or so it seemed. All that has changed in the past few years.

- The rise of China and India has gone beyond just providing cheap goods and call centres. The result is that the old patterns of power are changing and that is unsettling and possibly dangerous.

Brave new world?

Figure 4 Who owns the USA's debt?

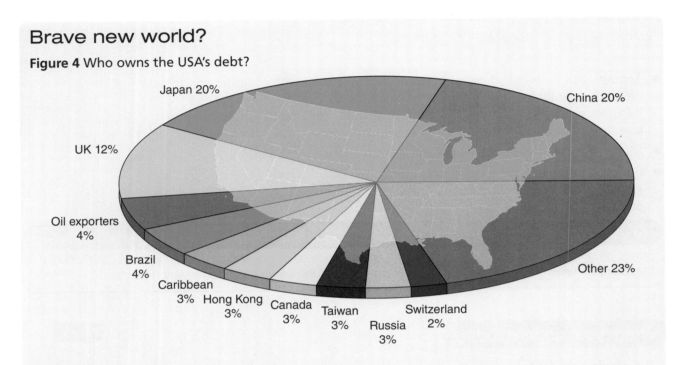

China

All governments have to borrow money to pay for public employees, such as the military, teachers and many others, while they wait to gather citizens' taxes. Most governments borrow by selling bonds. Bonds are a type of loan which is guaranteed to be repaid after a few years and to pay interest. Figure 4 shows who owns the USA's debt. China holds nearly a trillion dollars of this debt. If this debt were to be sold it could wreck the world economy.

We live in interesting times. The world economy is unstable and big issues surround the possibility of the emerging BRIC (Brazil, Russia, India and China) economies satisfying the demand for developed lifestyles and at the same time:

- meeting their resource needs
- limiting environmental damage
- staying away from conflict with neighbouring states.

At the same time, in the developed world different issues are pressing:

- how to provide jobs for people
- how to maintain living standards
- how to keep control of key research and development
- how to satisfy a population that may not enjoy the same standard of living as their parents.

And all the while …

- two billion people, mostly in Africa, south Asia and South America, live in absolute poverty.

Knowing the basics

Newly emerging **superpowers**, such as Brazil, are now starting to open operations in developed countries, changing the course of the global economy.

Stretch and challenge

The growing international debt, especially of the USA, has changed the balance of power. Maybe this is the end of the USA's domination?

examiner tip

The global economy is changing fast. It is fine to say that the future is very unpredictable, with a shortage of resources and competing superpowers.

Exam focus

1 State TWO effects of the greater integration of the global economy. [2]

2 Outline ONE feature of the 'new economy'. [2]

3 Study Figure 2 on page 72. Describe the changes in the gap between high-income countries and average global incomes. [3]

4 Identify ONE group that has benefited from the impact of the 'new economy'. [1]

5 Outline TWO reasons why companies may become transnational. [4]

6 The headquarters of most TNCs are in developed countries. Outline ONE reason why this is so. [2]

7 State THREE ways in which TNCs might bring benefits to developed countries. [3]

8 Explain why TNCs bring both advantages and disadvantages to developing countries. [6]

9 Define the term 'outsourcing'. [2]

10 For a named developing country, explain why it is attractive for companies that wish to outsource. [6]

11 Explain ONE reason why some people have a negative view of outsourcing. [2]

12 Identify TWO groups of people who might benefit from outsourcing. [2]

13 State TWO ways in which the workplace may change in the future. [2]

14 Describe how changes in skills might affect the location of some jobs. [4]

15 Explain why some people believe that global changes may not be sustainable. [6]

Answers online